BORN UNDER A GRANGE END STAR

David Collins

Published by Sigma Leisure – an imprint of Sigma Press, 1 South Oak Lane, Wilmslow, Cheshire SK9 6AR, England.

British Library Cataloguing in Publication Data
A CIP record for this book is available from the British Library.

ISBN: 1-85058-787-6S

Typesetting and Design by: Sigma Press, Wilmslow, Cheshire.

Photographs: David Collins, Rhys Collins ... and persons unknown

Cover Design: Design House, Marple Bridge

Printed by: MFP Design & Print

Foreword

By Phil Dwyer

When David first mentioned the idea of his book to me, I was intrigued. The chapters sounded interesting to say the least, and I couldn't wait to read the finished work for myself. As David expanded on his ideas to me, I simply knew he was onto a winner – and with a title like 'Born Under a Grange End Star', well he just could not go wrong as far as I was concerned!

As a Cardiff boy myself – a Grangetown boy to boot – I was proud to play so many games in the famous blue shirt of Cardiff City. I was fortunate to make it "through the ranks" at the club and ultimately ended up with the honour of captaining the side. Having been brought up within walking distance of Ninian Park – indeed I might well pinch the title of this book when I come to pen my *own* biography – I have witnessed the enormous passion which the club generates amongst its marvellous fans.

That passion and enthusiasm inspired me when I played for the club, and now it has inspired David to write, what I hope you will agree, is a thoroughly entertaining read. Sometimes hilariously funny, sometimes almost heart-breakingly sad, David tugs at the heartstrings in bringing to life the agony and the ecstasy of the life and times of a football supporter.

And such a shrewd brain too! Just read his selection of his all-time favourite Cardiff City XI, for example. But hey, I am giving away too much of the plot here!

Whether your lasting Ninian Park memory is scoring for your country against England in front of a full house, or missing Billy Woof's last minute winner because you left early to avoid the traffic, all the stories are here.

But even if you have never visited Ninian Park in your life, maybe never even been to a football match in your life, I think you'll still enjoy this endearing story of an ordinary Kaairdiff Kiddy, and his journey through life to adulthood, always clinging to that boyhood dream that one day, his team's turn will come.

One day David, one day.

Phil Dwyer
Ex Cardiff City and Wales

Preface

"Born Under a Grange End Star" tells one man's account of an obsession shared by many. It chronicles the development of a football fan, from babe in arms to full adulthood. All the joy and despair, the highs and – in my case – so many of the lows, are revisited.

Get in six cans of your favourite beer; any album by The Clash, and a pile of your old football programmes – and enjoy this rambling tale to while away a dark night.

It's really my own life story I guess, loosely based around a lifetime of supporting one particular football club. In my case, the club is my home town club, Cardiff City. But the story could really have been set in almost any town in Britain where a young man is drawn inexplicably by his dream for glory.

Though the work is deeply personal, I hope it will strike a chord with many. It will appeal to the armchair Premiership fan, who will smile at the obsessive behaviour of the antics of a lower division loony; the exiled Welshmen, who will remember so many of the names and places; but most of all of course, the book will ring true with dyed-in-the-wool football supporters the length and breadth of the country. The sort who finish work early to drive to Shrewsbury for a league cup tie, the sort who drag their kids to reserve games so that they can get autographs, and the sort who have to juggle the demands of school/wife/work/money, in order to fit in as many matches as possible over a long, cold winter on an open terrace.

I have tried to take the reader through events in a loosely chronological style. "Boy For Sale" starts in the early sixties and chronicles my own early influences. "Tank Top City" leaps into the fashion crazed 70s before plummeting to the bleak 80s. "Thin Blue Intifada of Happiness" brings us to the fanzine-dominated 90s, and "This is Tomorrow Calling" looks forward to my hopes and dreams for the future.

Yeah, the book is about Cardiff City. What did you expect? But stick with it, won't you? I look at football hooliganism; football songs and the fortunes of the Wales International side. There are matches you were probably at yourself. There are players you have never heard of. There is laughter and tears. There is hope and despair.

But most of all ... there is football, as it was always meant to be.

David Collins

For my Father

With thanks to:
Rhys – for helping with the photos;
Dan – for getting upset when Wales lose;
and Ceri – for putting up with the whole show.
i Cathy – diolch yn fawr am y teipio.

Contents

1.

Boy for Sale

I must have been a great disappointment to my father. No doubt, as I burst into life on a cold February night in Splott, Cardiff, 1959, his world was complete. His own career in the bare-knuckle world of Cardiff parks' pitches, so cruelly (as he never tired of telling me) cut short by injury, his ambitions were surely now set to rise phoenix-like from the ashes of a crippling knee injury/Continental Shift pattern. This boy, surely, could play.

Yes, as he paced the floorboards of my grandmother's terraced house in the shadow of the giant East Moors steelworks, waiting for the puff of white smoke (as opposed to the purple sulphur mist to which we were all so accustomed), I am sure that dreams for his son and heir filled his every thought.

A world where doors would open, scouts would linger and a tearful appearance at the end of 'This Is Your Life' a mere formality. Perhaps he would meet Danny Blanchflower … or Bobby Collins … yeah, Bobby Collins would be good.

Suddenly, as if by Magic Sponge on a cold day … he is straightened back to life. A baby cries! A nurse sighs and sales of season tickets soar. The proud father – shrugging off said knee injury – leaps the wooden stairs two at a time, hurtling along the dark, brown wallpapered passageways of the sprawling old house to welcome … the next Stanley Matthews? The new Lion of Vienna? A second Gentle Giant to play inside right alongside John Charles? "This time next year my boy … we'll be millionaires!"

Well something like that anyway. Next year, we did move some two hundred yards around the corner into Hinton Street, but never quite made it to Millionaires Row. And, as you might expect, I never did play the old One-Two with Big John to secure a famous Welsh victory over the old enemy at a packed Ninian Park.

Truth be told, I never even made it to the school team at my "Alma Mata", Moorland Road Junior School, a giant imposing Victorian fortress set amidst the rolling country-side of lower Splott, where St Patrick's Day was celebrated with as much hwyl as Christmas Day, Bonfire Night and your birthday all rolled into one. The Playing Fields of Eton? The Playing Fields of Splott Park perhaps, as every Thursday afternoon, after "Singing" (a curious lesson I always thought) we would snake our way, single file, through the long streets to the oasis which was Splott Park. A vast, blowy municipal open-air sports village, housing three football pitches, a rugby pitch, an outdoor swimming pool, two bowling greens and a children's play area. Sydney 2000? We could have held the Olympics in Splott Park in the summer of 1968, no sweat.

With a pair of six-studded, second-hand bovver boots slung professionally over my shoulder, along with about 100 other bright young things, I would wind my way the half mile or so to the brick-built changing rooms in the centre of our universe. It was time for the weekly Games lesson.

Well, all right, perhaps "lesson" is a tad strong. Forget images of some early FA School of Excellence, where a lean, track-suited student presides over a myriad of five-a-side games and brightly bibbed youngsters are encouraged to express themselves with a soft foamy football. Cue instead 20–30 scruffy nine year olds chasing a cannon ball across the Somme.

Not a replica shirt in sight as our "Games Master" (makes it sound like a posh school that, dunnit), the legendary

The author's father, in the baseball kit of Splott YMCA

Cardiff schoolteacher Bill Barrett, hopped from foot to foot clapping his giant shovel-like hands and roaring encouragement.

Though I didn't quite realise it at the time, Bill Barrett was to have quite an influence over me. A giant of a man, with a mighty quiff of white hair, his passion for schoolboy sport continues to this day. Football in the winter (it was always winter), with a brief respite for baseball in the summer. I was nearly 13 before I picked up a rugby ball. Made sure I put the bloody thing straight back down too, daft shape for a ball if you ask me.

Anyway, he was a colourful old character right enough, whose other passions included local history and art. On one cold March Saturday morning ... perhaps 1969 but I could be wrong ... Bill (or "Pop" Barrett as he was affectionately known) was livid with the entire team for failing to properly bring all his interests together by refusing to wear the paper "lucky shamrocks" made for St Patrick's Day by his art class.

I was crap at football and not much better at art, but Bill believed that, with a name like Collins, there must have been some vaguely Irish blood in me somewhere, so I was OK. I got good parts in the school plays, especially any which had an Irish theme, and went on many an archaeological trip exploring the old docklands of Cardiff. I think he was impressed by the fact that I was the only one to take a trowel on one of these excursions, rather than a 'uge pickaxe like the rest.

But it was at Christmas that he would really come into his own. Every year he would he stride the school stage like a colossus, to tell us the ghostly goings-on from Charles Dickens' Christmas Carol. I can see it now ... the mean, grasping, clutching old miser ... Scrooge that is, not Barrett, brought vividly to life with gestures and grimaces, voices and actions. And rounded off by displaying a portfolio of work painted by past pupils of Bill's art class, illuminating each scene in full and living colour.

I was rewarded for my enthusiasm for all this (not forgetting the influence of the County Cork moniker of course) by being offered the part of Ebenezer Scrooge in "Bill Barrett's: A Christmas Carol" – 1969 vintage.

Yeah, football; stories of old Cardiff; life in a Dickensian hovel. He was quite an influence I guess.

Well back to the school team. You know, the replica shirt bit isn't quite true, come to think of it. A classmate of mine, John Green – a most playful young urchin as I recall – managed to acquire a new kit, which happened to match the school's famous black and white outfit (black shorts, white shirts, black collar ... picture the 1966 West Germany kit and you're pretty much there).

This elevated young Green to near superstar status, and straight into the first team to boot. In years to come, loveable rogues of the game would pen autobiographies with titles such as "Have Boots Will Travel", though I have yet to see Green's "Have new shirt will automatically get picked for the school team" on the shelves of W.H. Smith.

My efforts at replica kit ran only to a pair of thick blue- and white-hooped socks – nice try Gran, but the lads played in black & white not blue & white, much like the old Arsenal socks from the "Ian Ure" period. Not the first time I was to be defeated in the old "replica kit stakes", more of which later.

Members of the school team were of course, heroes to a man. They would get all the best girls (even at 11), always get to play "Nervous" with the bustier ones, win all the fights and walk effortlessly into the baseball team as sports switched over for the summer term at Moorland Towers. However, in a display of ill judgement matched by Cardiff City's sale of John Toshack, or Sir Alf Ramsey pulling off Bobby Charlton in the 1970 World Cup quarter final in Mexico, Bill Barrett chose to overlook the new Lion of Vienna in one of his rare selection blunders. Or, I guess, it may have been because I was crap as well. You know that Alf Ramsey line about Martin Peters being ten years ahead of his time? Well, I was five minutes behind everybody else.

Author and parents; author wearing 'Hush Puppies' – honest!

So my role was to watch from the sidelines. Hmmm, I could manage this I thought, as Saturday mornings throughout the late 1960s found me on the muddy sidelines of Splott Park watching our brave boys wipe the floor with all the other 11-year olds in Cardiff. I had found a niche.

Yes, I watched gleefully as Moorland ruled the waves.

Well, ruled the parks anyway, as Billy Barrett's Black & White Army thrashed All Comers.

All that is, except Baden.

Local derbies have always had a special appeal haven't they? And Baden Powell Junior School were our nearest and dearest, local rivals.

Compared to the long dark streets of Splott 'neath the shadow of the steelworks, Baden Powell may as well have been set in the Cotswold countryside. For, despite the fact that it was only in nearby in Tremorfa – a low rise 1950s Council housing estate lying sort of between Splott and the Bristol channel – their "Garden Village" environment of front lawns, tarmac drives and cul-de-sacs seemed a world away from our urchin-littered rows of Victorian cottages, grey skies and all pervading smell of sulphur from the giant steelworks, which dominated our landscape. All Splott needed was a workhouse or a gang of dancing cockneys and you would swear you had wandered onto the set of some Dickens novel set to music. (You don't see dogs stuck together these days do you? This seemed quite common back then. The only cure being a bucket of ice cold water hurled by a Nora Batty lookalike from amidst a hoard of snotty nosed ruffians.)

To return to the story – Baden always seemed to hold the upper hand over Moorland Road Junior School in the late 60s. Their flaxen-haired young officer types in bright yellow shirts would effortlessly break my heart with gay abandon so it seemed, leaving our weary infantrymen to troop back across no man's land to their land fit for heroes.

My football watching shortly took the almost inevitable twist, as I soon found myself climbing into the cars of teachers and parents to go to away matches at other schools around the city as my classmates did battle in the noble cause. I was developing the early symptoms of Ground

Hopping. A trip to somewhere unpronounceable in Llanrumney sticks in the mind for some reason, while the "day out to end all days out" came in the 1969 final of some ancient schoolboy competition, probably named after the Marquis of Bute or the Chairman of the local Public Health Committee.

For this great day, we got to go to Corinthian Park, in swanky Llandaff (well, swanky Canton perhaps – depending on whether you're Buying or Selling) – for the big game against, of course, Baden Powell.

Ah, what a scene. The yellow-rosetted ones sat neatly 'neath the quaint wooden stand. Fagin's urchins banked high on a muddy bank opposite. Who needs Celtic and Rangers?

Sadly, our young lads froze on the day. Baden's resident superstar Denzil Lawrence (who later found fame as an international Kick Boxing Champion – I kid ye not!) scored two. Maybe three. My team was to blow it on the Big Occasion. A gang of diehards; a sea of passion; and it ends in tears. Ring any bells?

*   *   *

So there I was – confined by a lack of ability to watching from the sidelines. But outside school, that was a different matter. Outside I was George Best himself. Our street gang of 3–12 year olds represented all shades of the football fraternity. That is to say, we had one whose father supported Hull City, along with two or three Italians. I think "Ully's" mother was Dutch too, but I can't be sure – Total Football never really catching on much around our way.

No matter. Honour was fought for with frightening regularity as we kicked and chased our plastic footballs between parked cars or the tiny patch of green opposite my house known as "Moorland Gardens" (it means "church of the broken bottle" in Welsh). We would engage in never-ending games of "Sides" or complex variations of "Attack and Defence", but usually it was "F.A.".

Ah "F.A.". What memories of glory days gone by. Basically, this was every man for himself against one goalie (always Lesley Jones) in which we would each battle through every round with howling fervour. If you scored you were able to then sit it out until the next round, leaving the last two standing to fight tooth and nail to avoid an ignominious early cup exit at the hands of some would be Giant Killer like Salvatore Canatella ... who was younger than the rest of us. A bit like King of the Ring only with a ball. In fact, a lot like King of the Ring!

The whole of the football world was there. The sneaky lazy goal hanger waiting to pounce (Allan Clarke made a career out of F.A.); the tiny industrious midfielder battling to dribble around the bread van; cruel deflections of the ass of an Italian – no change there then – and a string of death defying dives at attacker's feet from Jones-the-Goals. I swear my mother called me for tea once just as the ball was about to land invitingly at my feet following a wicked deflection off the roof of Splott Library. Clive Thomas? Audrey Collins? Well, whatever.

Lesley Jones was a giant amongst men. Maybe because he was a year older than the rest of us, I don't know; maybe because he was bigger than the rest of us. But he was the first soccer superstar I ever encountered. Such was his prowess on the field of play (all right..."streets" of play then) that in most games he was banned from scoring a goal. In our multi-racial, socially inclusive, 10 half-time 20 the winner marathons, where Marquis of Queensbury Rules OK, the cry would often go up "Lesley Jones can only score with 'is 'ead!" and the golden rule was thus invoked.

As our crossing skills left much to be desired at such a

young age (still do!), poor Les – on those rare occasions when he would be allowed to play as an outfield player that is – would resort to scrambling the ball single-handedly through a maze of tangled legs and around a helpless keeper before crouching to nudge the ball over the line with the side of his head. In his autobiography, George Best speaks of his dream of performing such a stunt in the 1968 European Cup Final against Benfica. Our man Les seemed to pull it off most evenings.

After the others had gone home Les and I would engage in a curious hybrid of "three and in" where I would strain every sinew to get one, never mind three, shots past his elastic frame, as the sun set beyond the towers of the vast steel works away to our right. He was all the goalies you had ever seen. I was George Best, Jimmy Johnstone and anyone from the 1970 Brazilian World Cup winning side. Why can't life stay like this, eh?

*   *   *

Deflated then, by the news that I was not destined to fill the space on my mantelpiece set aside for my first Welsh cap, my father decided to plump for Plan B of my football education. Cue brass band, cue gritty Yorkshire accent, here we go with "Dad takes son to football match saga".

Ah. This was indeed, romantic stuff. What a picture we must have made. Father wrapped up hard against the cold harsh winter, waif-like son shifting nervously as he was about to take those first tentative steps into the real world. His tiny hand clasped by his giant father as the steel grey smog consumed all. Do you know that scene at the start of Oliver Twist where Harry Secombe strides the streets of old London Town alongside a trembling Mark Lester? That was me and my dad walking around to the bus stop in 1968.

With shiny schoolboy rosette glowing in the shadows, I

boarded the enormous burgundy and cream bus – probably even a trolley bus, yeah sure to be … or a horse drawn carriage even – anyway, as I boarded the … etc … who could know the impact that was about to be made on my young impressionable self. Having a Man United poster and a Celtic mug was all very well. But a bus full of real blokes going to watch Cardiff City? This was male bonding at its best. Couldn't we just go fishing instead?

Yes, at the tender age of nine, having reached an appropriate level of maturity, my initiation at Ninian Park was set for an evening at the second leg of the 1968 Welsh Cup Final, as Cardiff City took on the might of non league Hereford United. Nothing like starting at the bottom, eh?

John Charles appeared for Hereford, leaving my father in awe. Being little more than a tot, I could barely see this gentle giant of the game, but my father was over the moon. It was 30 years ago and he's dead now, but my father's pride in sharing the same stadium as his hero remains my overriding memory of the evening.

City won the match 4-1 to take the trophy 6-1 on aggregate. John Charles scored. I know all this, because I've looked it up. But I know that my father was in awe, because I was there. Sometimes you just *have* to be there.

And so, over the years, our regular spot became the floodlight between the Bob Bank and the dark and cavernous Grange End. How oblivious I was then, as to how my life would be changed, indeed almost taken over, by the events to unfold around these enormous structures. If I'd known, I'd have probably left at half time against Hereford.

Actual games have faded from the mind now (though for some reason I always remember Ian Macecknie in goal for Hull City) but simply being at Ninian Park as the sixties drew to a close, is a memory which lingers to this day. The malady lingers on, you might say. Well, you might. I was hooked.

The roar of the crowd. The smell of the grease from the hot dogs. And the crush to get in. I was able to take my feet clean off the ground without falling over, jammed in by a thousand eager punters desperate to squeeze between the tiny turnstiles at the Grangetown end of the ground.

The giant fences which criss-cross the modern Ninian Park were nowhere to be seen back then, and shaven headed masses of the infamous "Cardiff City Skinheads" would roam menacingly from their natural habitat on the huge Grange End, across the terracing in search of, well, who knows what, on the Bob Bank. (Why does the club's official literature always refer to it as the "Popular Bank?" I know of no one who calls it the Popular Bank. I digress.)

I was terrified even to look at these monsters, yet at the same time, found them fascinating. "Watch the Game!" barked my father as I gazed not at Ronnie Bird but at Big Frankie from Canton, while the endless army snaked its way past us in single file. It was to prove a defining moment. For the next 30 years, how many times were the fortunes of the players occasionally rendered incidental, as the obsession with what I wore to the game, where I stood, how I got there – with simply *being* a City fan, would one day become just as important as the performances of Albert Armour, Tarki Micallef, Billy Ronson or a thousand others.

Back home in Splott, I was quickly emerging as the budding City fan. All the local streets were named after Welsh towns – Aberdovey, Aberystwyth, Llanelli etc – and in nearby Milford Street, lived the Taylors. Freshly moved down from somewhere up Pontypridd way, for some reason which I have never quite understood, the valleys accents of Robert ("Taffy") and his younger brother John ("Little Taffy"! – honest) seemed to give them a greater claim to being a real city fan than the rest of our tribe. "Toshack!" yelled Little Taffy as he thumped an imaginary cross into the net to give

City the lead over Leeds or Arsenal in the upstairs of their tiny terraced house. I too, would dive gleefully through the night air to add a second or even a third, denied a glorious hat trick only by my sister coming to tell me tea was ready. I could have been spotted by City if we had tea at six instead of five.

But I got her back. She was older than me (still is) and alive to the fashion world. But did she really think that she could knit a giant blue and white school scarf and keep it untouched by human hands? A free City scarf for me to steal whenever I liked. I commandeered it for "the Cause" as the Irish say, and wrote "C I T Y" in blue felt pen across the bottom. Graffiti was only a question of time. The boy was becoming the teenager. The black and white, steely grey sixties were to give way to the full colour, felt pen, lip-smacking, thirst-quenching, relegation-battle, never-ending seventies.

I could hardly wait.

2.

Tank Top City

It's ever so difficult being a teenage boy. Girls have it dead easy. Grow tall. Ignore the spotty younger boys. Drool over the older ones. It's a doddle.

But for us lads – well – there's just so much to remember isn't there? When I was 10, I was able to recite all the names of the entire 1967 Glasgow Celtic European Cup winning side. I could probably still do it. Ronnie Simpson, Tommy Gemmill, Billy McNeil, Bobby Murdoch ... . This was pretty straightforward. But three or four years later, oh, it was a minefield. Football teams, pop records, rules of Subbuteo. The list was endless. Boys can't simply buy a record and have done with it. You're expected to know the intricacies of it.

The author, circa 1973. 'Groovy' doesn't even come close!

If you momentarily forgot the name of Mott the Hoople's vocalist (Ian Hunter), or Willie Morgan's old club (Burnley), you were a has been.

The first album I bought was "Slayed?" by (of course) Slade in 1972. It cost me all of £2.25 – two weeks of delivering papers in Tremorfa. I was asked what I thought of the album and replied "Oh, the singles are OK, the rest are not bad – haven't really played 'em much I suppose". Well, if looks could kill. My mates were appalled that I was not already intimate with every single track; that I could not recite great chunks of lyrics, or name the guitarist on track seven. Blimey, it's only Rock n' Roll!

I had some sympathy for them though I guess. A lot of my school friends seemed to have older brothers. They were therefore used to this "need to know" culture. Equally horrifyingly though, they had been brought up on a diet of "progressive" bands like Uriah Heap, Deep Purple and Pink Floyd. To a man they were Status Quo fans, and spent *all* their spare cash buying up the entire Quo back catalogue. Oh yeah, you had to call them "Quo", "Floyd" or "Heap" to be really cool as well.

I was having none of this. I had an older sister.

Every day, when I wake up, I thank the Lord I've a sister.

Instead of testosterone-laden heavy rock combos, our house swayed to the sounds of Jimmy Ruffin, Stevie Wonder and Al Green. I was brought up to appreciate the finer things in life, like Diana Ross. Each new Motown chartbusters album was awaited with child-like excitement. She taught me the reggae smooch! Who needs Emerson, Lake and Palmer when Smokey sings?

But you can't just leave it there when you're 14. Oh no, you're expected to go the whole hog. It wasn't too long before we (i.e. me and my sister) were buying reggae compilation albums featuring the likes of Jimmy Cliff and Desmond Decker. This was *massively* cool for 1971, I tell you. But it did put us firmly in the skinhead/suede head camp. So I had to sign up fully didn't I? My longhaired mates bought trench coats and loon jackets. I had a Crombie and brogues. My white 'patch pocket' Oxford bags (a snip at £4.99 from "Gwyns" upstairs in Cardiff market) completed the image.

I'd wear the Crombie to home games sometimes with accessories of matching Cardiff City scarf and sewn on Wales badge. My mate Nev lived in Hengoed. He assured me *all* the skins in the valleys dressed like this. I felt socially accepted for the first time in my life. In later years I had a feather cut and a purple brushed denim jacket. I thought I was Adam Faith in 'Budgie'.

And designer clothes? Been there, seen it, bought the T-shirt. A Ben Sherman T-Shirt to be precise. Black and white check. OK, my mother knitted the tank top but you can't have everything.

But there was one item that was absolutely essential to any self respecting Splott boy. The denim jacket – Wrangler and washed three times before wearing. Compulsory attire. I used to wear mine with a Man United badge and a small Welsh flag in the centre of the back (above the waist). I was sorted. Bring on the totty!

Now I suppose I should explain here. It's quite a picture painted isn't it? Rare reggae albums, trendy haircuts, well hard Splott boy made good. Well, there's a minor flaw. A technicality. Hardly worth a mention really.

Well, you see. I just wasn't hard. A bit of a wimp if the truth were told. I was skinny, little and hopeless at football. All my mates had hard-sounding nicknames like Joe, Uggy and Gus. I was "Weedy". No-one's going to spray 'Weedy Rules' on the back of the Grange End, are they? We wrote all the names of the Form 2-S "Boot Boys" on the blackboard in our Welsh class once. "Weedy the Boot Boy? " Not on, is it? And just try getting a game of 'Nervous' when you're name's Weedy! The macho culture has a lot to answer for, I can tell you.

Anyway, Slade and Mud gave way to Elton John and Rod Stewart. KC & The Sunshine Band and other "funk" artists supplemented Tamla Motown as I blossomed into a Young Soul Rebel. The sister moved to Llanedeyrn. Weedy left school. I started work. A job. Wages. Away matches!

For years, Bonehead (no-one seemed to go by their right names in our school) had tried to persuade me that I should go to away matches. I was hesitant to say the least. I had only recently plucked up the courage to start watching games from the back of the Grange End. This was a scary place, I don't mind admitting.

To those unfamiliar with Ninian Park of this era, the "Grange End" (named after the Grangetown area of Cardiff) was always the traditional home end, prior to its demolition for safety reasons in the late seventies. It was an enormous, dark, cavernous structure, full of wild beasts of the forest. Some with no hair, some with long hair, and many dressed in long white coats. The rest of course, in the obligatory Wrangler jacket, "skinners" (awful white canvas baggy jeans) and enormous boots. Scarves hung from every wrist. It was like the Ghost Train at Barry Island. I was mesmerised.

The very song "Born under a Grange End Star" was a complex remix of Lee Marvin's 1970 growling classic "Wanderin' Star", sung by a gang of absolute outlaws from the depths of this dark and intimidating enclosure. Lee Marvin would have been quite at home with this lot.

From the very back of the Grange End, it seemed miles to the pitch. Youths who knew no fear would climb up the rafters to stand high up in the roof structure. Those back on terra firma would bounce up and down on the ancient wooden flooring. The whole enormous stand would sway and vibrate. Blokes would loose their virginity underneath the Grange End. Fights would break out between "Cardiff

SATURDAY, JANUARY 31, 1976

VERSUS

ALDERSHOT

OFFICIAL

10p

PROGRAMME

Division 3 : Kick Off 3 p.m.

WEDNESDAY, 26th NOVEMBER, 1969

VERSUS

GOZTEPE IZMIR

KICK-OFF 7.30 p.m.

BLUEBIRDS

1/-
JOURNAL

---

at Ninian Park today . . . .

NEWPORT COUNTY

Division Three

Saturday, 28th December, 1985 — Kick Off 3.00 pm

OFFICIAL MATCH PROGRAMME - 50p

---

at Ninian Park this afternoon . . . .

SCARBOROUGH

Barclays League Division Four

Saturday, 23rd April, 1988 — Kick Off 3.00 p.m.

OFFICIAL MATCH PROGRAMME - 60p

BLUEBIRDS

7p

JOURNAL

WELSH CUP 4th ROUND

CARDIFF CITY

v

SULLY

Wednesday, 14th January, 1976

Kick-off 7.30 p.m.

A lifetime's wasted Saturdays, watching half-remembered football teams do battle

Boys" and "Valley Boys". And Bonehead expected me to go away with this lot?

Anyway, by 1975, I was ready to give it a try. My induction was set for Swindon Town-v-Cardiff City. Doesn't sound much does it? Read on. Boxing Day 1975. Bohemian Rhapsody was No. 1. Of course, I knew every word of it ... and the names of all the band, all their albums and, like all good teenage boys, was fully aware that all Queen albums were endorsed "No synthesizers". At the time, it just seemed important to be aware of such things.

The faithful Wrangler jacket was accompanied by a white, yellow and blue Leeds scarf (my father couldn't get blue, white and yellow – he hoped I wouldn't notice the difference) onto which I had sewn a 'Cardiff City Superfan' sticker. Twenty coaches must have left Ninian Park, and every one was full. Bonehead and myself sat quietly in the middle. Wild animals sat at the back. On disembarking in leafy suburban Swindon, the entire population of this fleet of coaches ran through the centre of the main street in a longhaired mass of denim and tank tops. For why? Who knows? But I ran with the crowd, intoxicated. On entering the ground, the home end had a strange look to it. The decorators had been in. The words "Cardiff City" and "Wales" had been spray painted in huge letters across the walls of the terracing. The entire away end sang for an hour and a half. City lost 4-0. I couldn't wait to go again.

The very next day, undaunted by such a heavy defeat I, along with over 16,000 others, happily turned up at Ninian Park to see our brave boys thump Peterborough United 5-2. What other team could lose 4-0 one day, attract over 16,000 fans to a third division game the following day ... and even run out 5-2 winners! 11 goals in two days. And they call it a wasted youth?

In those far-off days, it seemed all my mates were Cardiff

City fans. I think the entire male population of our class went to Crystal Palace for a famous promotion showdown in April 1976, where an Adrian Alston goal gave City victory in front of a crowd of 25,604. Impressive by third division standards.

I recall little of the actual game now of course, over twenty years later, but clearly remember the massed Cardiff choir singing the Welsh National Anthem and Joe's home-made "Mal eats Footballs" banner, in tribute to the big mouthed Crystal Palace manager of the day Malcolm Allison. I think he had also written "Mal loves Fiona" or something similar in the bottom corner, a reference to Allison's well-publicised encounters with movie star Fiona Richmond. See what I mean about teenage boys, you really had to know your stuff in our gang!

That famous season – 75/76 – I went to a grand total of 31 first team matches – including a specially arranged "friendly" at home to Bristol City in May 1976 to celebrate both sides' promotion, them to the first division, us to the second. In not quite the carnival atmosphere the club had anticipated (less than 6,000 rolled up to see City lose 2-1 with an aged Brian Clarke notching City's solitary goal), both teams entered the pitch kicking free footballs to the crowd to reward the loyal supporters. 31 games and a ball didn't come within yards of me, of course. Still, look out for a similar venture if Cardiff and Swansea go up together.

Since that Boxing Day outing in 1975, away games went on to hold a curious fascination for me. Some of the more bizarre outings at the time included Bristol Rovers in the Anglo Scottish Cup (August 1978 – I was looking forward to a trip to Celtic or Rangers ... and we get Bristol); Southend in the snow (FA Cup – January 1976; hid in a graveyard to escape local youths!) and in later years, pre-season friendlies at Cwmbran Town and Inter Cardiff. I hitchhiked to Wrexham in May 1980, took the wife for a romantic weekend in picturesque York (lost 3-1!) and once drove to Gillingham and back with a hole under the back seat of my car. Inevitably, it rained.

In more recent times, I boarded the supporters' club official minibus to Hartlepool, for a Tuesday night fixture in November. We set off at about noon and the tiny bus was full of absolute diehards in ill-fitting anoraks. Their main topic of conversation appeared to be the progress of their respective Fantasy Football teams. Now, I don't mind Fantasy Football up to a point, but not all the way to Hartlepool!

The weather was also against us that day. It was snowing hard by the time we got to Coventry, but we persevered, past Leeds, up and onwards towards the far north-east. The game was only called off 40 minutes before kick off as we drove through Darlington. That's one hell of a trek in a minibus I can tell you.

Later that season, I got a phone call at home from Tony Jefferies, press officer with Cardiff City Supporters Club. He informed me that Cardiff City Football Club had offered to pay for a free trip to the rearranged away fixture with Hartlepool, this time on a Tuesday night in February, and did I want to go. Why not I thought? The snow held off, we won 3-2, and I danced with Gareth Stoker's mum after he had scored the winning goal at our end. Two midweek trips to Hartlepool in the same season. Is this getting out of hand do you think?

By the eighties, the adolescent Gang of 30 had become the Gang of Two. But between leaving school in 1975 and getting married in September 1985, I doubt if I missed more than ten home games, with the giant "Sprukey" at my side for each one. If either of us were not directly beneath the cameras on the Bob Bank every other Saturday afternoon, then something was up. You name 'em ... we've seen 'em.

I have seen Cardiff City Football Club play every team in

ADAR GLAS CAERDYDD
SUPPORTERS' CLUB

SEASON 1978-1979

MEMBERSHIP CARD
SENIOR

the league at home except Liverpool and West Bromwich Albion. If you add on cup games and internationals, I reckon I have seen around 120 different teams at Ninian Park over the years.

Sprukey and I watched gleefully as Peter Kitchen rattled in five goals against Cardiff Corries at a midweek Welsh Cup tie in December 1980, rejoiced as Billy Woof swept home a late winner in his only appearance against Wigan Athletic in September 1982 and grimaced as City lost at home in the FA Cup to non league Weymouth three moths later. Why, we even took the afternoon off work to catch Peter Osgood's appearance for Southampton reserves against City's combination side circa 1979 – had to go in the Grandstand for that though as the club didn't open up our usual spot on the middle of the Bob Bank for reserve games. Where's their sense of tradition?

After a while, things just became ridiculous. Though we now both lived in Rumney, we would still meet back in the Moorlands pub in Splott after Football Focus but in time to watch the boxing (on the tele, not in the Bar), catch a City Circle bus which took us half way around Cardiff, to end up on exactly the same spot on the Bob Bank as last time. A pastie was, of course, compulsory. On the way home we'd both choose our own man of the match and then I'd make sure I was first in the local newsagents to buy the evening's Football Echo – in order to read every detail about a game I had watched in person barely an hour earlier.

If we lost at home, the entire plot was ruined until the City Circle began the cycle again two weeks later.

Away games were even more extreme, the selection of each trip being based on formulae which would have taxed Einstein, or even John Motson. Had we been there before? How far was it? Would we get a beer *and* be back in time for a swift one in Cardiff afterwards? Was it an important game? Would City win?

In order to be assured of a decent seat on the coach from Ninian Park, Sprukey and I would ... listen to this for a pala-ver ... each catch the Number 30 Newport to Cardiff bus (from different locations naturally), travel right the way across Cardiff to the station – including a walk down Tudor Road, turn up at Ninian Park at around 8.30am, only to head back across Cardiff via ... the road to Newport. Some weeks we'd go right past Sprukey's house!

But this itinerary took us to all manner of exciting outposts – Oldham (lost 2-1, Phil Dwyer scored); Orient (lost 4-1 with a Kevin Bartlett goal); Southampton (lost 3-2 – I think Robin Friday scored them both); Hereford; Swindon (again); Brentford ... but the only time our detailed criteria were fully met was during a trip to Exeter City in January 1983 – beer in a Devon hostelry beforehand, 2-0 win for City courtesy of Bob Hatton and Jeff Hemmerman and back in the Ninian Park pub by 8 o'clock – *and* Andrew Dibble signed my programme.

But it wasn't all welcoming West Country taverns and rambling strolls around sleepy rural outposts. Away travel with Cardiff City can be extremely hairy. Nightmares at QPR, Shrewsbury and Fulham spring readily to mind. Crushing defeats in the East Midlands, long journeys home from dark northern towns, perched on a railing at Torquay on a Wednesday night. It was bloody hard work I can tell you.

But the worst trip was easily Wolves in the dying days of the 1985/86 season – we were attacked entering *and* leaving the ground, City lost 3-1 in front of a mere 3,353 in the heart of the Black Country. In the vast decaying stands of the old Molineux, there were tears in our eyes. The local South Wales Echo told how there was no hiding in "Shadows of the Past". The result sent *both* of these famous old teams to the fourth division. It was the lowest of the low. And boy ... have there been some lows.

I attended only three league games the following season as my enthusiasm was tested to the limit. The reality of Cardiff City in the Fourth Division was simply unbearable. The match programmes summed up the whole sorry affair – an eighteen page journal featuring six pages of adverts, two pages of black and white photos and hardly any interesting reading material whatsoever.

"Division 4 Newsdesk" kept us in touch with fellow sufferers at Darlington, Doncaster and Torquay, whilst two pages of an August 1986 programme were dedicated to Rochdale, the first ever visitors for a fourth division game at Ninian Park.

Former City full back (sic) David Grant, one of "Durban's Donkeys" – or maybe he was a Len Ashurst "wheeler-dealer" – now turned out for Rochdale and he was featured in the programme proudly bearing a watering can symbol on his chest with the Sponsor's logo "All in One Garden Centre" written on the side of the can. These were indeed, embarrassing days.

I couldn't wait to grow up and put all this malarkey behind me. When I do, you'll be the first to know. OK?

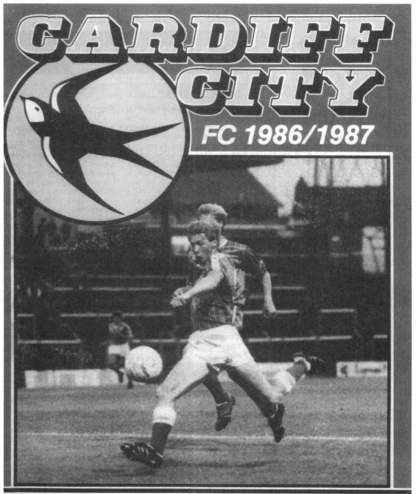

at Ninian Park today . . . .

ROCHDALE
Division Four
Saturday, 30th August, 1986 – Kick Off 3.00 pm
OFFICIAL MATCH PROGRAMME - 50p

Cardiff City's lowest ebb: starting a new season in Division Four, for the first time ever.

3.

Only a Game?

It would be extremely hard to pen any kind of account of the life and times of Cardiff City and ignore the question of football hooliganism. Like it or not, in some quarters, it is Cardiff's biggest claim to fame. It has brought the club national media attention over a 30-year period, affected potential investment in the club and generates much of the atmosphere in the ground. At many clubs, it seems to have gone out of fashion, but to many followers of Cardiff City it remains as much a reason for supporting the club as Sam Hammam; promotion prospects or the chance of FA Cup glory.

This chapter seeks not to glorify the issue, nor even to justify it. But perhaps we can explain it a bit. Why is there *such* a problem at Cardiff City?

To my mind, Cardiff has always been a rough place. I grew up in Splott in the 60s and 70s. Splott is rough. Believe me. Go there.

Then I moved near a Cardiff Council estate known as Llanrumney, then to Llanedeyrn. On the last bus home to Llanrumney, fights would break out based on the length of someone's hair. I was once picked on for being "a punk". Just because I had short spiky hair and a cap sleeved shirt. In Llanedeyrn, one of my sister's neighbours shot a dog. With a gun.

So I guess it might come as little surprise that Cardiff City fans enjoy – if that's the right word – something of a reputation for hooliganism. It's long established and fully deserved. When I attended my earliest games with my father some 30 years ago, enormous skinheads would patrol the ground. They came from the long, dark streets of inner Cardiff; the docklands of neighbouring Barry; and the tiny terraces of a thousand valley towns. An eclectic mix. A tapestry, woven together in a common flexing of community muscle.

But there's more to it than that. I have a theory about Cardiff City hooliganism.

When I first started watching Cardiff City in the late 1960s, the team was successful. The club attracted large audiences. Almost inevitably, the hooligans followed. In the era of Bovver Boots, flick knives and the Skinhead Moonstomp, it was the thing to do.

Then, virtually overnight, the team collapsed. Toshack went to Liverpool. City blew their chances of promotion, and a lifetime's relegation battles commenced. But that was just it. Panic set in. It has never gone away. Suddenly, the results of struggling Orient, Blackpool and Crystal Palace became matters of life and death. The last game of each season brought a tension you could not imagine. Relegation was unthinkable. But when it came, as it did in 1975 and 1982, City mounted a rousing promotion challenge to roar back, only to simply start the whole process again.

Consequently, almost every game I have ever attended has mattered intensely. The fact that crowds fell to embarrassing levels mattered not a jot. Cardiff City games became, almost literally, life and death to some people.

In rugby union, no one really cares who wins or loses. As long as it's a good game with some ridiculous score like 34-19, everyone is happy. Whereas in football, the actual game can sometimes be totally irrelevant. The performance is completely secondary to the result. Forget "15 man rugby" or even "Total Football" – just hurl it forward for Leo to bundle it in. We don't come here to be entertained!

I once travelled to Chester City on a freezing cold day to stand on a decaying, open terrace, where a desperately poor Cardiff City team fought out a 0-0 draw against a team who practically no longer exist. The ground is no longer used for football. The pubs were all closed. But I couldn't have been happier. That point helped us avoid relegation. Who wants to see a feast of football and lose 5-4?

Even defeats can be salvaged. How often have I poured over the Football Echo, sat glued to the radio or searched Teletext, in the hope that, say, Portsmouth have also lost, thus rendering our away defeat at Lincoln less of a disaster. Turning on Teletext to see the result of game where you do not already know the score is a nightmare. The right result can send you leaping around the room. But a late goal by someone you have never heard of playing for Mansfield against Notts County, can send you into depression for days. Multiply this by 42 league games, then by 30 years, and you start to appreciate the importance of Association Football to many people's lives.

If you have something of a general interest in football but don't happen to follow any one team in particular, you really cannot imagine the tension this creates. The number of meaningless games played by Cardiff City where I have been able to relax and simply enjoy the game, can be counted on the fingers of one thumb.

And so different people react in different ways. I used to come home and argue with my father. Now I sulk and shout at the kids. Many of the skinheads who followed Cardiff City in 1969 have grown up or grown away. But many stayed. Hooked on the drug. The prospect of failing to avoid relegation or secure promotion each year became unbearable to many, and they would lash out. I don't condone it, but I do understand it. Cardiff City is important. *Football* is important.

I once saw a handful of Cardiff City fans invade their own pitch in an attempt to break down the goals late in the game, and thus force the abandonment of one particularly painful home defeat. There was one away fan in the ground.

Of course, this is not the whole story. The ocean of passion has now spawned a life of its own. Mayhem seems to follow Cardiff City wherever they go. As the games have mattered enormously, armies of desperately committed young men travel the length and breadth of the country to feed their habit. But the monsters and raving loonies are now generally happy to go along with the image that they have helped to create. The whole thing has become a self supporting dynamo. For many City fans, "enjoy" really is the right word when it comes to their reputation for hooliganism. They even sing "We are the Famous Football Hooligans!"

The image first created in the 1960s was defended and upheld vigorously throughout the 1970s, as giants of the hooligan world fell from grace into the second division for brief periods. Chelsea, West Ham and Spurs came down. Bristol Rovers, Bristol City and Swindon Town were also still regular visitors. Millwall were often around. Cardiff City fans lapped it up. This was the Big Time. A real chance to rub shoulders with the big guns.

And who can forget 31 August 1974. Manchester United, the undisputed kings of seventies soccer violence came to town. United were in the Bob Bank. City on the old Grange End. I was in the Canton Stand. Bedlam. It was like something from an Orange Day parade on the streets of Belfast. One police officer on the Grange End wore a crash helmet. United won a featureless game 1-0. Legend has it that City chased United out of town.

Now then. Here's the key. Hands up all those who felt a

tiny bristle of pride at the thought of Cardiff City's infamous firm getting a result over Manchester United? Be honest. If I had said "United kicked the City Boys to pieces" I am sure there would have been a loud reaction from people saying "No!". "Get your history straight buddy".

A year or so ago, things went a bit bonkers up at Stoke. The events are well documented. I didn't go, but met someone I vaguely recognised from a thousand away trips on my way to the pub that night. He is far from being a hooligan, but told me that I could rest assured that the City mob gave a good account of themselves.

It's a hard thing to admit, but we *do* feel a sense of pride that the boys held their own, or even started things, when trouble flares. Test yourself. How would *you* feel if you heard a story that Swansea fans had run riot at Ninian Park and gave all our boys a good pasting? See, I even call them "our" boys. And I'm a million miles from being a hooligan I can assure you.

This all takes on a life of its own and goes off on a thousand tangents. Listen to the crowd at Ninian Park next time you go. The crowd is praised for its passion and support, the bulk of the noise coming from the Bob Bank. But listen to the songs. For every song in praise of Andy Legg or Robert Earnshaw, there's at least two declaring that "Engerland is full of shit" or waxing lyrical about past battles with Millwall or Bristol. At games against Gillingham the crowd is urged to "stand up if you hate Swansea" ... and they do! If it wasn't for the minority of football hooligans and, more significantly, those who are happy to go along with the image of it all, there would be virtually no atmosphere at many football games.

In some quarters, football rivalry is almost manufactured at times, simply for the sake of it. Peterborough hate Cambridge; Plymouth hate Exeter. But Cardiff City hate ... anyone they happen to be playing at the time. Even the defi-

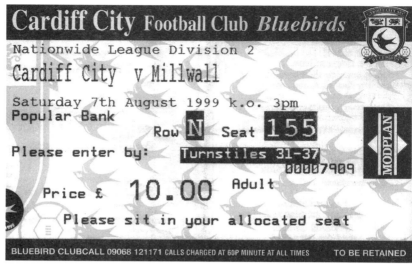

Cardiff City v Millwall. Just when you thought it was safe ...

nition of a local derby has been stretched beyond all reason as an excuse for running riot at some sleepy third division town. Hereford, Shrewsbury, Torquay? These are not "local".

I have seen large bricks hurled into piles of Burnley fans; hand to hand combat at Fulham; piles of debris thrown at Swansea City players at the Vetch; bottles thrown at Roger Freestone during a testimonial; heard ugly chants about the Yorkshire Ripper or opposing players who have committed suicide; and seen Argentinean flags displayed at home games against English teams. A two pronged pitch invasion against Luton in 1994 had to be seen to be believed. I heard rumours that CS gas was used. At a Wales international at Ninian Park in 1976 someone even threw a corner flag at a linesman! You wouldn't have thought this was physically possible would you?

The current generation of City hooligans has taken this to unprecedented levels. The Cardiff City "Soul Crew" seems to

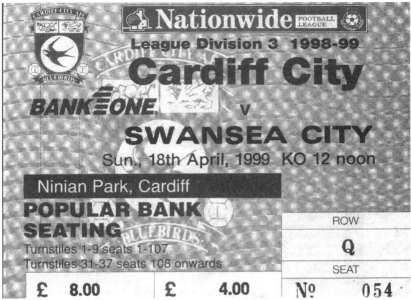

Cardiff City v Swansea City. Unbearable.

be a generic term applied to an eclectic mix of individuals who currently keep the pot boiling on behalf of the boys in blue. They have their own web site. You should see it. It's most impressive. It talks of "keeping the faith" and outlines the history, aims and objectives of the current mob. There are pictures of the crew in action. It's like something a small ambitious Local Authority would put together.

This all simply helps to fuel the legend of course. Although the former City director Ron Jones tells how Cardiff City's growing hooligan problem acted as a positive deterrent to investment in the club during the 1980s, there are many who see this as a positive advantage. It's hard to strike a balance on the knife edge between partisan and pandemonium. Yes, you want your home ground to be intimidating; you need to create an unwelcoming atmosphere to inhibit opposing teams – but then you can overdo it. Just cast your mind back to January 2002 – to the Cardiff versus Leeds game to see just how delicate the balance can be. At times Ninian Park is wild. Absolutely wild. Recent games against Millwall and Swansea have been simply terrifying.

And what is it with this Swansea thing? Why can Celtic play Rangers; United play Liverpool and Chelsea play West Ham ... but games between two struggling lower league sides have to be planned with military precision and away fans even banned for years?

I know why. It's jealousy. Go back to 1978. John Toshack looks set to leave Anfield and rumour has it that he is on route to Ninian. Tosh is asked about his coaching qualifications and the City board get cold feet, Tosh heads West to Swansea, City go into terminal decline. The Swans go up and up; waving us goodbye with a hearty two fingers on the way. Gone are the fond memories of cheering a victory by a fellow Welsh club. Forgotten is the bitter rivalry with Bristol City or Swindon. Suddenly it was "You Jack Bastard" and "Crack-a-Jack." *We* were supposed to be the Sleeping Giant waiting to rub shoulders with Liverpool and Man U, not them. For some, this was simply too hard to take. Welsh Civil War broke out.

And what about the Swans – how had they seen things? For years, Cardiff had been the big club; the so called media darlings. I have read that BBC Wales is known as "Bluebird Broadcasting Corporation" on the North Bank, Swansea. Suddenly, in 1980, the boot was on the other foot – and it wasn't coming off without a fight. Literally.

By the time both teams were back languishing in the lower leagues, the dye was cast. A generation of City fans had grown up hating Swansea and vice versa, without really knowing why. Don't get me wrong, I take great pleasure from victories over Swansea City. In fact, I hope they lose every game they play. I have no problem defending this attitude. Would you expect a Celtic fan to say "Yeah Celtic ... but I want all the Glasgow teams to do well". I think not.

So there you have it. The result is all. The boys get carried away. The boys enjoy it.

But CS gas, bricks and throwing corner flags? Is this really it lads?

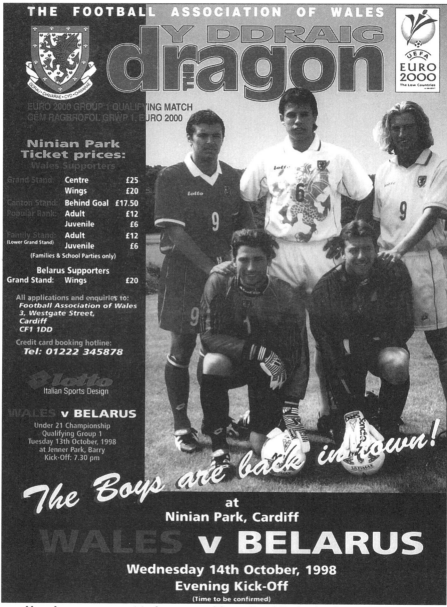

How is a guy meant to keep up with replica kits in the face of this lot?

4.

Y Ddraig Goch

If the passion and fervour I feel for Cardiff City could ever be matched, if some games matter even more than Mansfield versus Cardiff, then that honour rests on the shoulders of the Ddraig Goch. The Red Dragon. Hope springs eternal. Hope springs a leak. What a tale of woe *this* one is.

Sometimes, I believe that, if Cardiff City were in the Premier League, all would be well with the world. I ache for this every day of my life. But for just one day in the sun with Wales, I would cut off both my arms and legs. As Billy Bragg once said, "I'd walk a mile with a stone in my shoe. That's the price I pay for loving you the way that I do." I would die a happy man. But no. Clearly it is all, just too much to ask. Pam fi, Duw? Pam fi? *(Why me, God? Why me?)*

I yearn for it to be our turn. I want the rest of the UK to tune in as *Wales* fight out a tense penalty shoot out on a hot night in June. I want World Cup BBQ nights from Bala to Barry Island. I want mothers to cry as little Robert Earnshaw is booked for a silly foul and misses the final. I want a plastic Robbie Savage free with a packet of Frosties. I want to swap shirts with Brazilians, conga with Colombians and record a terrible song with Charlotte Church or the Super Furry Animals. I want it to be our turn.

Every year, I seethe with jealousy at Des Lynam. I hate Football Focus and Five Live. I even hate the rugby. For days, even weeks before some meaningless game of chase-the-egg, the Welsh media would have us think the whole thing actually matters. No one really cares about rugby. Ask a man in

Rhyl or Rhyader about Pontypridd versus Dunvant. They don't give a toss. Neither do I.

But what do I get instead? The Wales international football team. Oh little Englander, you will never, and I mean *never*, know.

Please don't sing to me about your 30 years of hurt. I have had 30 years of absolute agony, tragedy and heart breaking failure. Vital penalties which crash against the cross bar. Desperate last-gasp equalisers to shatter the brightest dreams. Terrifying defeats in obscure eastern bloc countries. Dubious refereeing decisions which haunt me to this day.

Oh, yes. I have suffered.

I have witnessed riots at Ninian Park and floodlight failure at Swansea. I have feared for my life amongst 50,000 Scotsmen at Anfield. I have seen Wales loose, win *and* draw at Wrexham. And oh, that night in '93 at Cardiff Arms Park ... the Theatre of Nightmares.

I will be 43 at the time of the next World Cup. By my reckoning, as things currently stand, I have around six or seven World Cups left in me, if I am lucky. Assuming that half of these are held in South Africa, Vietnam or some other place thousands of miles away, then it only leaves me around three or four shots at taking a transit across Europe to see our Brave Boys in action. And given also that the score currently stands at "Sad old author: 40 years; World Cup Glory: Nil" the chances of three trips in the next 40 years seem ... well you have to say they look slim don't you?

No matter, when you see a huge banner at the San Siro in 2036 saying "CCFC OAPs on Tour" then you'll know who's responsible won't you?

But still. I need to indulge myself here. This is meant to be a fun book after all. And yes, in amongst the lowest of lows, have been, occasionally, the very highest of highs. The nights we have danced. When mañana mattered not a jot.

Here are my two favourites. The times when, for one night only, all the dreams came true. When there were Stars in Our Eyes. Tonight Matthew, tonight I am going to be ... over the moon.

Of course, nothing's ever simple with Wales is it? Even in these rare moments of triumph, something crazy happens. Combine the emotion of International football, with the adventures of Cardiff City and you have a potent mix. Too strong for me at times. The first story is very personal. The next? Well, you were there, weren't you? Are you sitting comfortably? Then I'll begin.

* * *

It was 1977. The punk-rock scene was setting the world alight as my beloved Wales ventured to the twin towers of Wembley to take on England. "Do anything you want to do", they yelled. This was the Modern World. Like a fool, I went along with it.

The decision to embark on this fateful venture was taken whilst passing from The Horse and Groom public house to The Cottage sometime around Christmas in 1976. The air was festive, the world was gay (you could say "gay" then). Wembley in the Spring. What could possibly go wrong? The answer, excluding the actual game, was simply everything.

The three revellers who left The Horse and Groom that beer-frenzied Christmas, had dwindled to two by the time we arrived at The Albert at noon on Tuesday, 31 May 1977. The condemned men ate a hearty breakfast of pasties and brown sauce, complemented by Brains Dark (can't really buy Brains Dark these days can you?) before setting off to the dark streets of London Town.

We had, of course, decided to travel with Cardiff City Supporters Club. Proper coaches that promised a quiet drive to London. Yet on this mild spring afternoon, whilst walking to the pick-up point at Ninian Park, I made the worst decision of my life. A charabanc pulled up and Arthur Daley hung out of the window. On seeing our scarves, we received a warm invitation to board and travel to the game at a most haffordable "knock-down" price. A bargain for two fine gents such as your goodselves. Ahem.

So, should we trundle on down Tudor Road as planned, full of Brains Dark, or accept the offer to join this friendly looking outing from Barry? You guessed it. We climbed aboard. Oh dear.

It soon became apparent that the entire coach was pissed. The first official toilet stop was at Howells Garage in Newport Road. I made this eight minutes of actual travelling time. Soon, some of the wildest men in Barry were standing outside the coach watering the wheels in the broad daylight in the middle of the busiest road in Cardiff. In those far-off primitive days, in-coach toilets were unheard of. As we set off again, the driver, who later was to play such a major part in the proceedings, invited us in future to urinate out of the coach's open door as we sped along the M4. The contents of many bladders were emptied along the motorway to the accompaniment of "Scarlet Ribbons" from the back seats. I looked around me cagily. I had joined the official outing of

1977 – way back when, fans wore scarves

Cardiff City's Barry Boys. Monsters to a man.

Our next stop was Chievely Services on the M4. As we alighted, the Barry Boys introduced themselves to their English cousins. Within seconds, one was completely naked and staggering around the service area. A frail old lady picked her way through the debris. The shop was completely emptied. Not a penny changed hands. I thought I was going to die.

Now amidst all this chaos it should not be forgotten that this was to be one of Wales' greatest footballing days, a trip to the twin towers no less. As we crawled to the ground, those famous towers loomed in the distance. They glowed majestically as we neared the fabled ground to park up for the evening. We made our way to a conveniently situated pub. A giant football-shaped ashtray was collected as a souvenir, though I swear I never saw a soul go inside.

Shortly, as the Boys relaxed outside the tavern, a coachload of Englishmen turned up, complete with the usual gestures and insults. A Barry Boy was on their coach in a flash. Veggie. Veggie removed his front teeth and entered the coach, determined to remove someone else's. He returned toothless but unscathed and we left for the ground. I was absolutely terrified.

Presently ... .we spotted familiar faces from the old Grange End. A Harlequin swathed in colours of the rainbow. The Flagstealer's tale unfolded. Our man had been spotted with an England flag about his person. Youths from Wales had set on him. But no. Flags and scarves of all colours hung from every wrist and our young cabellero returned the blows with interest for even thinking he was English.

I was being enlightened by the minute. We paid £1.50 entry, made our way to the Welsh end and looked out on to the hallowed turf. Ah, a glorious sight! Three days earlier, Manchester United had beaten Liverpool in the FA Cup Final and now Don Revie's men were about to entertain us. They were full of household names; we had Joey Jones and Dai Davies. Another five had turned out for Cardiff City at some time or another: Leighton Phillips, Rod Thomas, Dave Roberts, Bryan Flynn, and Peter Sayer. Not forgetting Gabalfa bred, Terry Yorath, the midfield captain who held us together. Nick Deacy was up front, remember him? Wales battled and battled, cheered on by a healthy Welsh contingent.

In the 42nd minute, Peter Shilton fouled Leighton James in the box. A penalty. James himself stepped up and fired the penalty home. Wales were winning 1-0. Say this quietly to yourself. To date, this was the greatest moment of my life.

All the pretend matches I had played against England in the streets of Splott were coming true. I had scored hat-tricks in all these matches, let me tell you that, but on this occasion I was more than willing to accept the solitary goal as victory tonight. For the rest of the game I chewed my fingers and personally cleared three efforts off the Welsh goal line. Dai Davies took years off my life saving certain equalisers. Terry Yorath was everywhere. After a lifetime of whistling, I saw Peter Sayer throw his arms in the air and other Welsh players jumping for joy. Wales had beaten England at Wembley. Heaven.

England 0, Wales 1. Match ticket signed by Terry Yorath, Leighton James and Joey Joes. Arguably my proudest possession.

Now if the Barry Boys were lively before the game, imagine their glee as the scent of victory filtered through their nostrils. They sped from the stadium to spread the word to all and sundry. My own personal fortunes took a backward step at this point as two disgruntled home supporters set upon me while I was searching for our coach. They whipped off my scarf and, frankly, kicked my head in good and proper. I thus made the wise decision to quit the ring there and then. My record, fought one, lost one, a sound testament. "I could have been a contender." Perhaps not.

Finding our coach was rapidly becoming a full-time job. Numerous others had left the ground, leaving familiar faces in the rapidly emptying car park. The warm spring afternoon was now a cold, dark night. The unbelievable had happened; the driver had left without us. He had had enough and gone back to Barry, leaving us high and dry.

Fear not lads, there's the Barry Boys over there (oh, no!). They had got their second wind and were busy diverting traffic with temporary road signs. A nearby exclusive hotel was visited and the majority of the residents informed of the result by the Barry Boys. The Met Police were now on hand. As we had so far managed to keep a low profile, I suggested to my fellow traveller, the luckless Gary, that we take God's speed to the train station. He agreed. We hitched to Paddington down the Harrow Road but there was not a lift in sight. We caught a taxi to the train station, and arrived virtually penniless. It was awful.

Paddington at midnight is short on entertainment. It's cold and lonely and there's no talent. But fear not, for the night was far from over. Through the misty night air emerged … the Barry Boys. Like a recurring nightmare. They had come in search of the "milk train".

Does this mythical vehicle actually exist? Is there really a train offering free lifts, warm milk and a cosy bed to dishevelled travellers in the dead of night? In a word, no. The next train was at 7am. It was 1am. It was cold and I was on a station platform with 40 hooligans. Think about this when you're tucked up in bed tonight.

So Ali Baba and his forty thieves roamed the platforms of Paddington for six hours. Apart from us, the place was deserted. We were almost penniless. The lads were restless. As we huddled on a cold, hard British Rail bench, Gary assured me we would laugh about this one day. I never have.

Eventually, at around 6am, the ticket office opened and we inched a step nearer to home. Our finances stretched to two half fares to Cardiff. (We'd worry about the ticket inspector later). At seven we were, indeed, in heaven. Back on the train home, and despite the accompaniment of 40 other oversized fourteen-year-olds, I had never been happier.

It had been a long, long night, and the cracks were showing. My scarf had gone. My dinner was still on the coach and I had lost a jumper. The fight in the car park was beginning to ache. I had been to hell and back, and returned with a 1-0 victory. I got off the train in Cardiff and went straight into work (they weren't pleased). That night's Echo carried the front page headline "Disgrace to Wales Fans left behind." I hid it so my father wouldn't see it.

I was to be at the next three England v Wales games and we lost only once. There were 70,000 at Wembley in 1979 when Dwyer played, and in 1983 I met Ian Rush. But somehow it was not the same. We got home safely from each game after this and never again made the headlines – carefully planned mini buses from The Albert saw to this. Wales never won again. I never got lost or beaten up, and I never had the company of Veggie and the Barry Boys again.

Thank God.

* * *

So you see, I have suffered for my art. But my football-watching ventures aren't always this bad. Usually, but not always. Sometimes, there have been those rare moments, those rare nights, when the result was what we hoped for; the game went well; no-one was locked up and the beer was cheap. All right then, maybe there was just one night ...

*   *   *

Cardiff Arms Park. 1991. The greatest story ever told?

It all started calmly enough. Seats had been booked well in advance for an all-ticket affair in the works' social (The "City" club would you believe?). Beers and a chat before the big one against the Germans. Thirty-eight thousand people in Cardiff for a football match, there was no way I could miss it. No way at all. I was determined to enjoy every minute.

Four o'clock found me comfortably sat in The City club (only 80p a pint), cosily sipping what I'd promised to be the first of merely only one or two gentle pre-match looseners. Five or six gentle looseners later and the mighty Arms Park beckoned – the call of the wild, Westgate Street, thronged. Flags and scarves all around, hot dog vans, the lot. Could this be our night? Could this be the one?

Inside the ground the atmosphere was overpowering. The anthem boomed out. Hymns and arias demanded a Welsh victory. Behind us the biggest banner I have ever seen proclaimed "Cardiff City, Wales, Bluebirds" along three giant red and white stripes. There must have been twenty fellas holding it up.

Whenever I watch big matches on the TV nowadays, I turn to my young son and assure him, "One day it'll be our turn, son, and you watch us go." Tonight was our turn. The whole of Wales was there.

Amidst this ocean of passion, a football match was taking place far beneath us. Cagey and nervous Welshmen pitted against the slick and assured master race. Brehme, Voller, Matthaus against Rush, Southall and Ratcliffe. It was electrifying.

The Germans stroked the ball about on the smooth Arms

Park pitch. Barry Horne hit the bar. The last match I had attended had been Cardiff City v Maidstone. It seemed a thousand miles away.

The enormous Germans moved freely, always a man in space. Mexican waves sprung up under the giant stands. A bad sign. The hwyl was dissolving. A guy in a Wrexham shirt urged more noise. I responded with The Ayatollah, frenzied slaps on the head falling on deaf ears. Matthaus pulled down a cross with the most marvellous piece of skill I had ever seen. It wasn't going well.

In the second half, as a thousand urine streams flowed into the waters of the Taff, Berthold booted Ratcliffe and a bright red card changed the course of history. The crowd exploded. We would never have a better chance and the team knew it. A previously tense Paul Bodin found Ian Rush in space and in front of goal. The keeper stayed put. A bulging net, and I was thrown into the air. Four of us fell over in a line along the back of the seats. I clawed my way to the gangway to stand rigid, scarf held aloft, Wales shirt gleaming brightly under the night sky. The whole ground was going bananas and the Germans couldn't take it. Their easy "beach soccer" of the first half became an irrelevance as Andrew Melville thumped the ball clear, Mark Hughes charged and challenged and Neville, well, Neville….

The intensity of the crowd was becoming alarming. The Wrexham shirt was blue in the face. My leg sported a three-inch gash from I know not where. At the final whistle, it could have been amputated from the knee and I would not have spared so much as a downward glance. I was delirious.

I abandoned my seat in a race towards the pitch, only halted by the fact I was some twenty yards above it. Undeterred, I took to beating the boards in ecstasy as the Germans silently folded their flags. I hugged a total stranger. He hugged me back twice as hard. He could have been the leader of The Pencoed Jacks for all I cared. For

Wales v Germany, 1991. Oh! How we danced!

once, the whole of Wales was united. Awful night games with City were a distant memory. Anfield 77? Suddenly they all seemed worthwhile as a lifetime's wasted Saturdays found their justification. This is why I watch football. Close to tears? I was close to ejaculation.

Racing out of the ground in glee, I seized a discarded South Wales Echo cutting – "1-0 to Wales – Says Yorath" the headline. Holding it aloft like Moses with his tablet of stone, I danced and sang uncontrollably. If the guy who took my photograph is reading this, I hereby offer a thousand pounds for a copy of the picture.

Back at The City club the air was heady. Nobody thought about whether or not Wales would qualify. Tonight you're mine completely. We had beaten the best team in the world and we had all played our part. I began to drink myself into oblivion. Next season I would be at Crewe and Barnet, but today, today, we had beaten the world champions. Oh! How we danced!

*   *   *

As I suggested at the outset, I have been dealt so many crushing blows by following the Wales national side, that picking out these two "highs" (if being stranded on Paddington station can be regarded as a high!) was a fairly simple task. The only other contender was Wales' 4-1 defeat of England at Wrexham in 1980 – arguably the most enjoyable whole day of my life.

But life will go on. Long after I have hung up my replica shirt and sat down with *People's Friend*, others will carry the mantle. Others will endure the heartache, tell their friends and drink to forget. Some may even write stories of their adventures in far-off lands.

Well, for those who *may* choose to wax lyrical in text in the future, I have prepared a template. An easy guide to follow. So, "Dear Writers of the Future: Please find attached your very own Cut Out and Keep World Cup Press Cutting". Guaranteed to suit all occasions. As they say in the Civil Service – Delete as Appropriate, and watch the years roll agonisingly by ...

"More Welsh Woe in World Cup Washout"

The woeful Welsh wizards once again lived up to their tag as the Nearly Men of world soccer last night at:
Ninian Park
Anfield
Millennium Stadium
TNS Llansantffraidd

Roared on by a huge crowd, the luckless Welsh needed only to:
Beat
Draw
Turn up at the right ground

against
Scotland
Iceland

Romania
Isle of Wight

to move towards next year's finals.

Despite a tough group including
(Insert here name of current World Champions)
(Insert here name of quick-passing East Europeans)
(Insert here name of minnows with dry, dusty pitch miles
from anywhere)

the qualifying stages had seen a series of battling
performances from the injury-ravaged side put together for
the campaign by
Mike England
Terry Yorath
Bobby Gould (heavens no … not again, please!)
Tony Wilcox

Welsh veteran
John Toshack
Ian Rush
Craig Bellamy

earning what will surely be the last of his 50 Welsh caps,
almost gave Wales the lead but his agonising shot
hit the bar
was somehow saved by the part-time Lithuanian goal-
keeper
finished up in Ely

Referee (insert own name) of
Germany
Iraq
Argentina

mystified the huge crowd and the TV audience watching on
S4C
SKY
Carlton
Red Dragon Radio Video Phone-in

with curious interpretations of the
Handball laws
Offside laws
Line-out laws

After 56 minutes, tragedy struck when speedy winger
"Ynpronounsobul" beat luckless
Joey Jones
George Berry
Daniel Gabbidon

to cross for "Nefferurdovim" to beat
Dai Davies
Neville Southall
Roger Freestone

with a dipping volley that
took a cruel deflection on its way to the net
slid agonisingly under the unsighted keeper's body
my granny could have saved.

There was more drama in the second half as Wales hopes
were once again dashed in the now traditional cruel penalty
incident, as
Welsh striker is brought down
Referee spots mysterious handball by Welsh defender

and *either:*
Terry Yorath
Paul Bodin
Robert Earnshaw

tamely hit his shot at the keeper; *or*
Don Masson
Davie Cooper
Hagi
... any other player you care to mention!

finally sealed Wales' fate from the spot.

But the night will surely be remembered as much for the
off-the-field drama as
the floodlights failed
ugly violence erupted amongst rival factions in the home
crowd
the opposing manager collapsed and died

and security problems at last night's venue mean that
Wales will play their next match at a different venue.

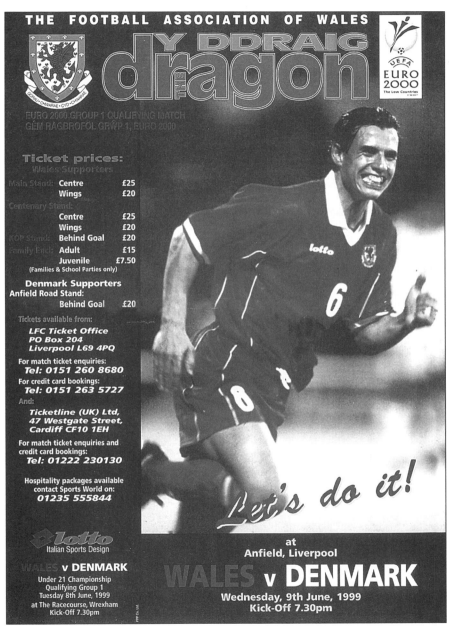

Wales have played three times at Anfield; this is the only one I missed.

Financially lucrative options under consideration by the cash-starved Welsh FA include
Anfield
Anfield
Anfield

After the match, Welsh stars called on the FAW to end the current uncertainty surrounding the manager's contract by giving the job to
Mike England
Terry Yorath
Gabby Yorath

on a permanent basis.

To complete a miserable night for British football, England went down 1-0 to the Shetland Isles, leaving Poland and Turkey to qualify from their group.

5.

They Brayed in Blue

A h, now, here's a good game. "The All Time Cardiff City Top XI". Manager, Yours Truly. Money no object, as I build the perfect dream team.

This chapter took me ages to write, I don't mind admitting. But what fun it was. So many memories, so many great goals, great players. So many afternoons I wish I had saved my money and stayed home and watched the racing on tele.

Read on ... let the Good Times Roll.

An empty stadium, but who cares? The author contemplates his dream team from the Grange End.

1. Ron Healey

The Eighties. Bleak. Bleak, bleak, bleak, bleak, bleak.

War in the city. War in the country. Wah inna Rhodesia. Wah inna South Africa. Depression all around. Inner City riots. Cardiff City riots. No roof on the Grange End. No people on the Bob Bank. No cash in the tills. This town was coming like a Ghost Town.

But, a hero was to be at hand. To give hope to all. A light in our darkest hours. Thatcher? Mandela? Gorbachev?

Healey.

The claim to the title of City's most popular goalkeeper of all time is open to some debate. Cwmbran-born Andrew Dibble has his admirers. Georgie Wood had no hair, but we didn't care. Gavin Ward. Roger, Roger Hansbury, Roger. Good guys all. But for me. It has to be Ron.

Ron Healey was signed in 1974 for £20,000 from Manchester City, for whom he had made his debut as an eighteen year old and played top flight and European football, after a spell on loan. This of course, was back in the days when the club occasionally signed players you had actually heard of.

Ron competed with Ulsterman Bill Irwin for the top spot before making the position his own in the late seventies and, as I say, through the early eighties, maintaining what often seemed like a single handed never ending relegation dogfight.

Before the days of Sky TV's day-glow world of continental goalies, Ron's rosy red jumper stood out on some very grey days indeed.

For example, in one bizarre morning kick off against Cambridge in 1981, City ran out 5-4 victors. (Not the only time I have seen City share nine goals with the East Anglia side). After, I was stood next to Ron in the players' bar. I was cautious about chewing the fat with a man who had just conceded four goals at home, but decided to go for it.

Ron had, as ever, played a blinder, in what was Len Ashurst's first game in charge. One save in particular stands out when he blocked a point-blank header with stunning reflexes. Though I had marvelled at his dexterity, Ron modestly explained that it was simply a case of "watching the ball". Simply "experience". Eeee, I was impressed.

Only 3,243 souls witnessed this master class though I'm afraid. At the time, City's lowest league gate since the war. Like I say. Bleak.

City had long since turned relegation battles into an art back then of course. Look at this:

1977/78: a 2-1 victory over Notts County in a cliff-hanger of a final; home game, eventually secured safety after being a goal down.

1976/77: City scramble a point in the final game against Carlisle – to send Carlisle down in almost an exact replica of the events of 1974 against Crystal Palace.

1980/81 season ended with Ron keeping three successive clean sheets against Grimsby, Derby and West Ham. This left City in 19th place, separated from relegated Preston North End only by goal difference.

Ron had performed the same feat in the last 3 games of 1978/79 (Bristol Rovers, West Ham and Wrexham), coupled with a breathtaking penalty save against Sunderland's Wilf Rostron in the last away game of the season. All of which had seen the Bluebirds rise to the dizzy heights of ninth, temporarily abandoning the long established tradition of escaping relegation in the final home game of each season. Much needed respite for my overworked calculator.

As you can see, it was hard work supporting Cardiff City in those days – a clear head for maths being essential for the dedicated City follower. Most people remember the long lost summers of their childhood in scenes reminiscent of an Enid Blyton novel. My adolescence was one long winter where the Famous Five were City's back four with Ron Healey in goal.

Despite ongoing injury problems, Ron regularly cut the mustard in a struggling side. For those who like their meaningless trivia, I have it on good authority, that Ron was a tad superstitious. In particular, I hear that he was fond of touching both sides of the tunnel before running out onto the pitch. Dunno why. One of his rivals for the goalkeeping spot, Peter Grotier, liked new studs and laces for each game. John Buchanan was always first to get changed. Keith Pontin was always last. Good book this, innit?

It wasn't quite all doom and gloom in Ron Healey's day of course. In City's memorable promotion season of 1975/76, the former Man City man conceded just a single goal in the last *nine* games. In 1980 he kept a clean sheet against Arsenal in a cup tie watched by over 20,000 at Ninian Park. And that same year, Ron's heroics throughout the late seventies and early, bleak eighties were eventually again recognised by the Republic of Ireland. Remember this night?

Having been born in Salford, but of Irish parents, Ron had gained his only other cap against Poland in 1977. But cut to February 1980 now. Ron is brought off the Wembley bench to guard the sticks against the English. The full media spotlight shines on a guy with a bad back who plays for us. I was elated as he darted across the hallowed turf. Ah, glory at last!

Then, of course, disaster. The curly headed scouser has left our man stranded with the most audacious of chip shots. It was a classic. A goal destined to feature in a thousand "Keegan documentaries" for years to come. Little Ron's place in history is secure … the man chipped by Keegan. The heroics of a thousand games against Wrexham and Orient deleted in an instant. Life sucks sometimes, dunnit?

2. Linden Jones

Wing backs. What's that all about? Is it a winger, who can't tackle? Or a defender, who gets caught upfield too often? I've never quite understood.

In the days of "proper" full backs, there'd occasionally be one famous for overlapping. Terry Cooper, Carlos Alberto. That kind of thing. That was fine. When a Brazilian cracks in the greatest goal of all time on a hot night in Mexico City, nobody minds. But when Steve Grapes is asked to push forward away at Lincoln City, well – it doesn't quite have the same ring to it does it?

Ian Rodgerson, Andy Kerr ... even Josh Lowe. They ... well, they just make me nervous that's all.

Now Linden. That was more like it. Thick set, 5' 6" tall, unshaven, no real pace and the youngest player ever to be sent off for Cardiff City. I'm going to like this guy, I thought. He plays like I do.

In 1980, a mate of mine rang me from our works staff club to say that Linden Jones was there, playing pool. Lord knows what he was doing in our staff club, but I was gutted that I couldn't make it. So my buddy got him to sign a beer mat. It says "To Dave Collins, second-best right back in the world, from Linden Jones". I still have it.

Yeah, Phil Bater, Joey Jones, Linden Jones. Me. Proper full backs.

That dismissal I referred to above, came in only Linden's second game, aged 18 against Blackburn Rovers, for throwing a punch. Like much of Ron Healey's best work, Linden's heroics coincided with desperate relegation battles between 1978 and 1983. His never-say-die attitude, served us so well. He even scored for me once, when I visited Notts County for the opening day of the 1979/80 season. Sadly, though, we lost 4-1! "Get back and defend Linden!".

Actually, I am doing Linden Jones a bit of a disservice here aren't I? Spotted playing for Bargoed YMCA (a kind of valleys version of Bocca Juniors), Linden was a tough yet accomplished defender whose unshaven appearance gave him the nickname "werewolf" amongst his fellow players. A man who, curiously, always liked the same meal before each game, he became a lynchpin of the side during the early eighties, before moving on to Newport County in a bizarre 5-man-swop deal where they got Linden, Tarki Micallef and John Lewis and we gained Nigel Vaughan and Karl Elsey.

His particular success during the 1983 promotion season – a gem of a year following an uncharacteristic unsuccessful attempt to avoid relegation the previous year – was such that his talents earned him a full international call-up. The Aberbargoed-born slugger even made it to the squad for the Ninian Park friendly against Brazil in 1983 when 35,000 souls squeezed in on a roaring Sunday afternoon (the last football match I attended with my late father by the way). Sadly, that full cap always eluded him though, but his picture appears in full colour in my match programme alongside greats like Zico, Socrates and Gordon Davies. (Socrates signed my programme incidentally. I went to Ninian Park the day before the game and saw him getting off the bus. That's the team bus of course, not the number 19 from Llanrumney, which I used to use.)

If Linden had played in that game, I think he would have been up against the flying Brazilian winger, Eder. Linden Jones marking Eder? That would have been worth seeing.

3. Jason Perry

I'm not a great one for meeting my heroes. I once met Ian Rush outside Wembley in advance of a Wales/England game in 1981. "Gonna score a few tonight then, Ian?" I asked excitedly.

Rushie came back quick as a flash in that wisecracking,

loveable young scally-the-scouser style for which he is so revered. "Yeh, 'opefully."

So no, I am not a great one for lauding it with the players really. In my youth, George Best's role was to smile down from the purple walls of my sister's bedroom, wearing a pink Sergeant Pepper T-shirt. This he did with much aplomb of course. But if we had seen him in the flesh, propping up a blond somewhere, it might have coloured our view beyond repair. Nah, never meet your heroes – you might be disappointed.

But there are exceptions. Why do I feel that I am a personal friend of Jason Perry? Is it perhaps because I recognise in him, so much of the style and poise upon which I had based my own game as a slow recovering right back for Pentwyn Dynamoes Old Boys, and a host of Sunday morning Showers?

Like Joey Jones, but perhaps without the pace, I would patrol the right hand side of my muddy patch like a lazy guard dog, hoofing it into touch with gay abandon. "Out Pentwyn OUT!" I would yell as my fellow defenders lumbered forward in a crude and ineffective demonstration of the art of the off-side trap.

Was Jason the younger brother I never had? The protégé I never spawned? I had taken kindly to him ever since he made his debut as a 16 year old in March 1987 – an otherwise unmemorable season in which City finished 13th in the old fourth division in front of average gates of around 3,000.

If you are ever lucky enough to visit the 1927 café in Splott – a positive shrine to the Bluebirds as you might expect – you'll see a cracking picture of Jason Perry stood over Swansea skipper David Penney in a Vetch derby from the late nineties. The same picture was on my son's wardrobe door for ages, along with one of Ryan Giggs and Bart Simpson.

I think that part of Jason's appeal lay in the fact that he

played with the grit and determination that we would all display, if ever lucky enough to grace the hallowed turf. His Up and At 'em/They Shall Not Pass fervour made him a cult figure on the Bob Bank where his attitude was to earn him the nickname "Psycho".

Always a bit unfortunate that nickname I felt. When an uncertain ref is weighing up the pros and cons of a poorly timed tackle – was it a bad foul? is a yellow card in order? – half the Bob Bank screaming "Psycho! Psycho!" suggests a degree of "previous" doesn't it?

But Jason was as close to the fans as any Bluebird ever was. It seemed to *matter* to him when City lost. No wonder we were so close.

It damn near broke my heart when Jason moved on to Bristol Rovers. I simply couldn't imagine a City side without him. How would I cope? Oh, I had lost loved ones before – Gordon Owen, Andrew Dibble, the Bennetts – but I always thought me and Jason were, well, special like.

I heard a story once that Jason's least favourite ground was Bristol Rovers (I find it hard to even take that lot seriously at all) so I was especially hurt when he left our sunny shores to go play in a cowshed.

I put this to Jason on the touchline during Jimmy Goodfellow's testimonial against a Manchester United in later years, having invaded the pitch from my seat in the Junior Bluebirds' enclosure to get his autograph "for my son". As I thrust our autograph book into his hand, I pleaded with him to shore up our leaky 4th division defence. "Love to mate" he said. Jason Perry called me "mate". Did you spot that?

I once wrote to Steve Borley asking where I could put my hands on a Jason Perry testimonial shirt (as worn in the testimonial game against Spurs). Borley personally brought it to my house on his way home – he lives not far from me – and handed it over in exchange for a contribution to the youth team's funds. I wear it to this day (my wife hates it). Steve Borley suggested I could ask Jason if he would sign it for me. Hmmm. It's a tempting thought.

4. Rod Thomas

Ah, now. This has surprised you hasn't it? A lean and cultured defender in amongst the hoof it and hatchet men.

I used to drool over Rod Thomas. Amidst the journeymen cloggers and loan transfers of the Cardiff City sides of 1977 – 81, "The Fox" stood out like a beacon. A Brecon Beacon, even. Cool and accomplished. Tall and graceful. Fifty Welsh caps. A true artist.

I always used to try really hard to like any Welsh players in the City side back then. I never warmed to Tarki or Ray Bishop, and even Dave Roberts was never quite the hit I had hoped. More just "Hit and Hope" I guess.

But Rod? A pearl. Born in Glyncorrwg (don't ask), City had snapped him up for a bargain £10,000 from Derby and he made his debut in a 2-0 success against Stoke City. By my Tremorfa maths, City's £1m Stoke man Graham Kavanagh should therefore be 100 times better than Rod Thomas. If he is, I am buying a season ticket tomorrow.

Rod Thomas had graced the full back spot for Wales and Swindon playing in the same 1969 League Cup winning side as one F Burrows. Former City boss Bobby Gould scored in the final for Arsenal of course. Who says I haven't researched this book at all?

Championship success came his way with Derby County in 1974/75 and so Rod brought an alarmingly impressive CV to Ninian Park. Though a sweet full back, it was in central defence that he most caught my eye. Reading every game with poise and perfection, he would stroll effortlessly around the edge of the box, bringing balls under control with

those elastic spidery legs of his. The perfect foil for the more
– ahem – "robust" approach of Keith Pontin, Phil Dwyer or
Paul Went.

So, was he yet another potential "manager who got away",
or simply one more faded has-been seeing out his career?

Well, for me, definitely the former. In a similar way in
which Kevin Ratcliffe brought much needed poise to the
abrasive young hopefuls of Eddie May's championship side
a decade later, Rod Thomas both slotted in and stood out in
more desperate days. Rod left the club in season 1980/81
aged 34, to join near neighbours Newport County. (You
could assemble a half decent side from City players who
have left to join Newport County). When Rod left for Somerton Park, Newport, I also made the short journey to witness
his debut, against Walsall I believe. I used to visit Somerton –
easily the worst ground I have ever been to – quite often in
those days, blissfully unaware of how the fourth division
dungeon would one day become oh, sooooooo familiar to
me.

In Rod's day, international sides ran under 23 sides,
though I have never understood why 23 should be regarded
as such a watershed in a player's life. Rod appeared at this
level, of course, before making his full debut as far back as
April 1967 against Northern Ireland at Windsor Park, Belfast
(I didn't go). Dave Mackay – who could play a bit himself
mind (ask your dad) – so admired the cool youngster that one
of his first moves as Derby County boss was to fork out
£100,000 for the tall, fierce-tackling defender who had
served him so well at the County Ground, Swindon.
£100,000 was a tidy sum for a defender in those days,
remember. That puts the price of £10,000 City forked out in
some context. Defenders like Rod are a rare breed even now,
but in the relegation haunted seventies and eighties ... well, I
don't think we really knew just how lucky we were.

5. Phil Dwyer

To be honest, this is a bit of a hard one. It's not that I don't have much to say about Phil Dwyer, it's just that, well he's such a part of Cardiff City folklore, that everybody knows all the stories already, don't they?

The infamous "death by tongue swallowing" at Gillingham in 1975, the heroic goal against England in 1978, the awesome strength, the goals, the grimaces – "Joe" is, quite simply, part of Cardiff City history. Along with Keenor, Toshack, Don Murray and a handful of others, one of the few who could justifiably claim the crown of the greatest ever Bluebird.

All the facts and figures about Joe are very well documented – ten full caps, six under 23 caps, over 470 league appearances.

Phil played at right back for most of his career with Cardiff City, but to be honest, he was something of a Jack of all trades (sorry about the "Jack" tag Phil) and played in any number of positions. Renowned for his fearsome approach, his tough tackling served him equally well as a midfield "enforcer" or a robust old-fashioned centre forward.

But you don't play all those games and win ten caps for Wales just through being big and ugly. His skills were recognised by many a fine judge and his versatility brought him international caps in midfield (Turkey), up front (England), and in a number of defensive positions, including clean sheets against Scotland (3-0) and England at Wembley (0-0). Make no mistake; this boy could play all right.

The Scotland game remains one of the highlights of my international career. I had watched the events of Anfield '77 from the back of the Kop engulfed by wild, ferocious Scotsmen. It has taken me years to stop hating Scotland after Joe Jordan and his countrymen had cheated and terrified me. Even now, the only games I grudgingly want Scotland to win are against England. To this day, I hate Joe Jordan with a passion. When he signed for Man United I was gutted. When he was sent off at Swansea against Wales in 1981, I cheered and gesticulated as wildly as anyone else on the North Bank that day. Me, cheering happily on the North Bank at Swansea? Who'd have thought it?

Anyway, I simply could not resist the lure of seeing a Cardiff City player play for Wales at Wembley Stadium. And so, I made my second trip to the twin towers in 1979 only a few days after the Scotland game at Ninian Park.

Cardiff City at Wembley – what could possibly go wrong? World War III was taking place all around me as half of London seemed to be mixing it with City diehards. I was a scrawny 20-year-old, ill-equipped for hand-to-hand combat. A huge banner to my left proudly sported the Prince of Wales feathers on a red and yellow background as I peered through the debris. Sticks and bottles rained down through the entire game, but I saw our hero blot out the English threat in the manner to which I had become accustomed. Stirring stuff, eh?

And so. I have Joe at centre half in my best ever line-up. That's Linden Jones and Jason Perry as full backs, with Joe and Rod Thomas in the middle. This is what my friend Dianne would call a "robust defence". Mind you, she is a lawyer.

Rod Thomas narrowly edged it over the great Kevin Ratcliffe for the "smoothie" role on the basis that he played more games, a tough one to call though I admit. Linden just about shaded it over another "proper" full back, Phil Bater and Jason Perry would simply have to be in any side selected by me.

As for Dwyer, well, could you imagine such a side *without* Phil Dwyer?

6. Doug Livermore

Like many other clubs, City has probably signed the odd duffer here and there. The Godfrey Ingrams, the Billy Woofs, Nigel Stephensons, Chris Marustiks. Yeah, we could all reel off a few I'm sure.

But sometimes, sometimes, they get it right. The handful of successful seasons over the last 30 years have usually coincided with the shrewd acquisition of a seasoned old campaigner who's done the business at a higher level.

Just think about it. 1983 Promotion – Bob Hatton. 1988 Promotion – Alan Curtis. 1992 – Ratcliffe and Robbie James. A good youth policy is all right of course, but there's just no substitute for experience.

I never quite warmed to Jimmy Andrews y'know. He was never going to be the charismatic, high profile manager I craved when I was 15. I wanted George Best as player manager! But no, we get a quiet talking Scot I had never heard of.

By all accounts though, Andrews was a top coach and, through a canny knowledge of the transfer scene, secured golden boy Tony Evans, former hero Brian Clarke and the highly influential Mike England. England joined on a free transfer from Spurs and played 40 league games in 1975/76 as City raced to promotion from the old third division, a rock at the back alongside unsung hero Albert Larmour.

But it was Livermore who was to prove the most astute buy. Signed from Norwich City for £18,000, the Liverpool-born midfielder had made over 100 league appearances for the East Anglia outfit and starred in their 1973 League Cup Final defeat against Spurs.

Like Mike England, Livermore also featured in around 40 games for City that season, scoring three goals – including a remarkable diving header in a never-to-be-forgotten crunch game against Hereford United. A staggering 35,547 squeezed into Ninian Park that April night, when Dougie's goal brought the house down. He finished the match in style as well, setting up fellow midfielder Alan Campbell for a simple chance to seal victory moments from the end. 35,000 for a third division game. What was that about a Sleeping Giant?

Livermore played over 35 games the following season as well, scoring once in a 3-2 defeat at Oldham, before eventually joining Chester City for £12,000 in 1977/78.

His influence as the experienced hub at the heart of that 1976 promotion side can never be understated. Sometimes thought of as no more than a "fetch and carry" player, the term barely does justice to his expertise, guile and experience. Having started under Bill Shankly at Liverpool, it came as little surprise when he later assumed prominent coaching positions with Wales and then back at Anfield.

Livermore's influence had been immense, but he was allowed to slip away, to become just another name on a long list of managers City never had – Mike England; John Toshack; Kevin Ratcliffe and, of course ... George Best. Hey, a guy can dream can't he?

7. Willie Anderson

I guess I was always likely to pick Willie Anderson wasn't I?

Think about it. It's February 1973, days after my fourteenth birthday. My hair is comfortably below my ears. Rod Stewart records begin to fill the house. City, of course, continue to struggle at the foot of the second division. All is well with the world.

Suddenly, as if by magic, a man appears. A famous man, as Cardiff City splash out a club record £60,000 for Aston Villa winger Willie Anderson.

This can't be right, I thought. A man who had made his debut as a 16 year old for Manchester United (yes ... THAT

Manchester United) and moved to Villa for £20,000 was set to make his debut for us away at Swindon Town. I was amazed. I had *heard* of Willie Anderson. His picture had been in Shoot and everything! What on earth was he doing playing for us?

Willie Anderson was the sort of player you simply don't get nowadays. He would hug the touchline, shoulders hunched, ball stuck to his toes, "jinking" (no one "jinks" these days do they?) his way past mesmerised defenders. Long black hair and designer stubble – years before George Michael invented it – he had officially been marketed as "George Best's understudy".

Cardiff City want to sign George Best's understudy? Fine, I thought. Fine by me! A star was born.

Time plays tricks and 1973–1977 were not, as you will be coming to realise by now, Glory Glory Days for the boys in blue. No matter. We had a Pop Star in our team. Girls fancied Willie Anderson. I dabbled with a "Willie Anderson haircut", even though Ninian Park housed the National Collection of feather-cuts in those days. Willie was our hero. A pin-up. We made up a song – it went something like "Oh, Willie Willie ... Willie, Willie, Willie, Willie Anderson!" OK, I know, I know. It's not a classic by any means, but this was 1973 remember. The Jam and The Clash were still years away.

Amazingly of course, City's band of struggling battlers turned into world beaters for a season. Well, 3rd division beaters at least. The system was simple – Livermore wins it; passes it to Buchanan, who feeds Willie. Willie beats man, crosses ball, Evans flicks it home. Willie wins Supporters Club Player of the Year. I get a B in my history O level. Everyone is happy.

But by 1976/77, the tide was turning. The new wave was beginning to form. The old rockers had had their day. Willie left Ninian Park and moved to USA, having spent a summer there in 1975 (I went to Devon for my holidays – he goes to Florida!). Legend has it that Willie Anderson was as popular in America as the great Pele.

Pele? Understudy to George Best? "City Star in NASL Boom?". All this elevated Willie Anderson to superstar status as far as I was concerned. I had been used to Derek Showers, Roger Hoy, Mel Sutton. My father knew Ritchie Morgan's dad, and I thought *he* was a celebrity. But this. This was different.

Yes for the angst-ridden teenager seeking glamour in the Glam Rock era ... tell them Willie Boy is here.

8. John Buchanan

I bought one of those trendy retro shirts recently. You know, the old "blue-with-white-and-yellow stripe" from the 70s. A classic kit if ever there was one.

I showed it to a mate in work who is around the same age as I am, give or take a year or two. "Oh I remember that kit", he said. "John Buchanan!"

That was an unusual choice I thought. John Buchanan? His name wouldn't have been the first to spring to mind, I thought. I would have thought most people would have recalled the likes of Tony Evans, or Adrian Alston. Even Robin Friday perhaps. John Buchanan, though? Hmmm. Read on.

City wore that kit from 1975 to 1980. Remarkable by today's standards. But, the 1976 promotion party apart, the late seventies was not, by and large, a period of growth for Cardiff City. Relegation dog fights and last gap escapes. Gates were falling, Ronnie Moore not scoring. Centre halves playing up front ... they even knocked down the Grange End in 1977.

Dingwell-born John Buchanan joined the club from

Northampton Town for £30,000 at the very beginning of this period. His debut came in a wild 3-2 home victory over York City in 1974. I recall watching that game from the unfamiliar surroundings of the old enclosure in front of the grandstand – just yards from where someone threw a cup of tea over the ref!

He scored in his next two appearances and went on to regularly feature in the scoring charts over the following seasons, reaching 54 league goals in total, his feats including finishing as top scorer with a mighty 10 goals in 1977/78. Ten to be top scorer – we were that crap!

He topped the charts again the following season with a respectable 16 and even banged in 8 goals in a friendly against Rhyader in April 1980.

It wasn't just his feats as a goal scorer that brought him acclaim, but also his all-round ability and enthusiasm for the cause, earning him the Player of the Year prize in '78 and '79.

John Buchanan was one of the few City players to have his own terrace song, along with other all-time greats such as Tony Evans, Jeff Hemmerman and Dave Bennet. As I recall, it went something like "John Buchanan; John Buchanan – La La La La La" to the tune of a highland reel. All right it ain't exactly Lennon and McCartney, but when he has just cracked in the winner from 20 yards in some desperate rele-gation tussle (or the only goal in a 6-1 home defeat to Shef-field United!) you'll sing anything.

Though renowned for his dynamite-like shooting over some 250 games, one of his more memorable feats came by virtue of something of a tap-in.

City had been drawn at home to Wrexham during the memorable FA cup run of 1977. Wrexham were no mean side back then, and over 28,000 filled a noisy and partisan Ninian Park as local lads Sayer and Giles gave the Bluebirds a 2-0 lead within an hour. All went well until the northerners stuffed in two very late goals at the Canton End to pull level. Their huge, hairy striker Billy Ashcroft had bundled in the equaliser in injury time and I can still see one gleeful Gogg ringing a giant bell at the front of the Canton End. I wanted to ram it down his throat!

Steve Grapes shuffled forward down the City right. The game was over. I glumly contemplate the long coach trip to North Wales on a Tuesday night in February. He knocked it inside. How would I afford the bus fare three days after a big cup tie? Suddenly ... the mother of all celebrations erupts around me as John Buchanan – he of the dynamite boots – has calmly side footed the ball home in front of an astonished Grange End. Buchanan went bananas. He was not alone. If I were asked to name my five most memorable City games of all time, this would be right up there, along with the 1988 Welsh Cup win over Wrexham at Swansea; a 6-1 FA Cup hammering of Bristol Rovers in 2000 and a bizarre 2-7 home defeat once upon a time at the hands of Cambridge United.

But, of course, no story of the wonderful wee Scotsman would be truly complete without mention of *the* goal. The greatest goal ever scored? Probably.

City had abandoned the great 70s kit for a very dull plain blue ensemble with white collars. December 1980 – the bleak mid winter that was to last a decade. City v Swansea. John Toshack's lads were on a high. City were accelerating into a slump from which they have really yet to recover. It's minutes from the end, and City are 3-1 down. 10,000 joyful Jacks in the Grange End. This was going badly.

Peter Kitchen turned and scrambled in a consolation goal for City with moments to go. But the City fans in Ninian Park's largest gate of the season (21,239) still feared the worse. "Christmas won't be Christmas without any presents".

The rest, as they say, is history. An indirect free kick 300 yards from goal is gently tapped sideways, for Father Christmas to wallop the ball home ... in front of an astonished Grange End.

Ah yes. John Buchanan, John Buchanan.

La La, La La, La

9. Jimmy Gilligan

I wish clubs wouldn't mess about with their away kits. City's change colours have always been yellow as far as I am concerned. This is why that fantastic kit from the 70s had a yellow stripe down the side. In the eighties, I actually purchased a reversible nylon jacket which was blue on one side and yellow on the other. The ultimate utility garment – suitable both home and away.

All my T-shirts were blue or yellow. I bought a reversible blue and yellow scarf from the club shop. Sorted. I was kitted out for life. Then they changed to red.

Yes, the killer "replica kit bug" had struck again. In 1976 I had bought the dayglow red/yellow/green Wales kit – easily my favourite ever shirt. Later I bought the matching shorts. And the scarf. We even made a huge red, yellow and green banner for Anfield '77 (Wales v Scotland).

Then in 1980, Wales changed to simply red and white – leaving me with a wardrobe of useless clobber.

When the bug struck again years later as City went from yellow to red, the only thing for it was to unpick the yellow side of my reversible blue and yellow woollen scarf. I swear to you that I actually did this. Then, when my first son was born eleven weeks prematurely in December 1988, I asked the nurses at the University Hospital of Wales in Cardiff, if I could hang up my well-worn, half-a-scarf in his incubator. Amazingly, they declined. Something about germs. Women!

But I was determined that my boy would be a City fan. Instead of nursery rhymes, I would lull my lad to sleep with popular Bob Bank chants of the day. My wife says the baby's first word was dada, but no. My son's first word was "Gilligan".

I knew I was going to like Jimmy Gilligan the moment he joined the club. "Jimmy Gilligan." It just *sounds* like a footballer's name doesn't it? Like "Bobby Charlton"; "Bobby Moore"; "Ronnie Moore". Not like "Jamie Redknapp". Jamie's not a footballer's name is it?

Signed from Lincoln City for £17,000 in 1987, 24 year old Gilligan proved an instant hit. On his debut, he headed home the equaliser against Orient, then scored the winner against Swansea City in the next home game.

A 6'2" striker who knew where the goal was. Coming after the likes of Rob Turner, Paul Wheeler and Graham Turner, this was almost too good to be true. But no, City raced to promotion ... Jimmy banged home 26 goals.

As far as I could make out from my regular spot on the Bob Bank, the system was fairly simple. The pacey Kevin Bartlett (himself the scorer of 14 goals that year) would fly down the wing and whip it in for Jimmy to bang home with ease. Three in the last five games helped City to five consecutive wins. He also managed a goal against Wrexham at the Welsh Cup Final at Swansea.

So in October 1988, European nights returned at long last to Ninian Park. After an 11-year absence of continental opposition, City played host to Derry City, in front of 6,933. Not exactly Real Madrid but who cares. This was my era and I could finally lay the ghosts of Toshack and Clark. Jimmy Gilligan scored a hat trick. He also scored two in the first two minutes against Swansea on Boxing Day 1988 and grabbed an injury time equaliser at The Vetch. His place in my heart was secure forever!

The winner away at Bristol Rovers in February 1989 was a typical Gilligan strike. Roaring in between two defenders, controlling Bartlett's cross on his chest and then slamming home his nineteenth goal of the season.

26 goals last year. 22 goals the next year. Promotion. Winning the Welsh Cup at Swansea; European Glory – what was the world coming to?

This, of course, simply could not last. The form of Messrs Gilligan and Bartlett was said to be attracting interest from such giants of the game as QPR and Bristol City. Mighty Bradford bid £300,000 for Jimmy, whilst Bartlett had already been sacrificed to West Brom for a give-away £125,000.

Jimmy Gilligan had observed the proud traditions of the club by saving City from relegation with a goal in the penultimate game against Chester City but frankly, he was a gem in a poor side. I yearned for the days of second division dogfights against Crystal Palace as relegation to the 4th Division loomed again. How could the great Cardiff City be playing league games against Barnet, Maidstone and Scarborough I asked myself. Ten years ago, I had barely heard of these places.

As Frank Burrows left the club for Portsmouth, Gilligan soon followed. I followed as well, as two of us drove to

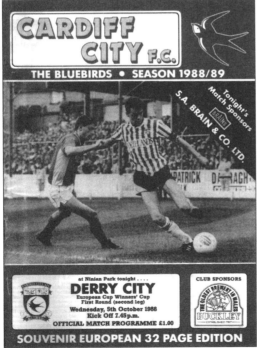

Jimmy Gilligan's finest hour?

Oxford to see Jimmy make his Pompey debut away at the Manor Ground. I even wore one of the hundreds of blue shirts from my wardrobe to fit in with the Pompey faithful. In later years I saw Jimmy play against Pompey for Swansea in a pre-season friendly at The Vetch (I have a bit of a thing about Portsmouth). Swallowing hard at the sight of Jimmy in a Jack shirt, I recall dancing uncontrollably as Pompey ran out 2-1 winners. Great night!

But, as they say, what goes around comes around, and in November 1991, City were drawn away to Swansea in the FA Cup. (Me – "I'll have to go!" Wife – "you won't". Me – "I WILL!")

So the Wild West again played host to another twist in the Gilligan legend. Half of Cardiff massed behind the goal at the crumbling Vetch. An immense police presence steered everyone to the ground on special buses. Someone threw a brolly on the pitch and City fans pinched the ball – only to toss it back on while Nathan Blake was about to whip a cross in. The usual Cardiff/ Swansea shenanigans then. Chris Pike bundled in the opening goal and I think they equalised with a penalty. But, as sure as night follows day, this was to end in tears.

After 57 minutes, Jimmy the Jack picked up the ball some 20–25 yards out. He advanced forward … to unleash a cracker into a bulging net. The level of inevitability surrounding this is hard to explain. The City faithful sighed agonisingly. We had seen it all before. The Jacks, of course, went mental to a man. They had knocked City out of the FA Cup and one of the greatest former Bluebirds of modern times had scored the winner – at our end. Jimmy span away gleefully to a packed and delirious North Bank.

It was all too much for me. Sometimes I hate football. My son is a teenager now and can say lots of words apart from "Gilligan". One day I will explain all this to him.

I wonder if he'll understand?

10. Carl Dale

As Mark Aizlewood would say, "You have to say" (he always says "You have to say"). City have not been well blessed with nippy little strikers over the years.

One glory season from Tony Evans apart, the likes of Peter Kitchen, Ray Bishop (Ray "the ferret" Bishop by the way – I have a fascination for nicknames), Tarki Micallef and Steve Mardenborough have been, well, ordinary at best.

Big Fellas – not a problem. Gilligan, Hemmerman, Toshack, Alston – every couple of years or so City seem to stumble across a reasonably effective big guy. But little 'uns, less success I am afraid.

Oh there's been the odd chink of light here and there I guess – Gordon Owen, Jason Bowen maybe, perhaps even Robert Earnshaw, but it's not a hatful of riches is it?

Apart that is, from one wee man.

Signed from Chester City by Eddie May in 1991 for £90,000, 5'9" Carl Dale was one of the first, and easily one of the best, pieces in Rick Wright's magic jigsaw. Even if we did lose the picture and fail to complete the puzzle!

The Colwyn Bay born striker was, quite simply, a diamond, with a phenomenal goal scoring record in what was largely – 1993 apart – a desperately grey era.

Dale was arguably one of the most underrated players in the lower leagues. Don't forget he had scored 41 league goals in 116 games for mighty Chester City. And from the moment he arrived with us – courtesy of a typical poacher's goal on his debut at Crewe – little Carl was a hit. He went on to rattle in 27 goals that year in a side which finished ninth in the old fourth division, plus the winner in the Welsh Cup final, to finish joint top scorer with the much maligned Chris Pike.

Even though Dale missed much of the glorious 1993 promotion season due to a knee ligament injury (was this the most enjoyable season of watching Cardiff City since 1976, I wonder?), the former Arsenal schoolboy still managed 17 goals – only two behind Pike again. But to be truthful, Dale was three times the player Pike was. He would harry defenders, chase back-passes, follow up rebounds ... it was like having three centre forwards sometimes. In fact, Carl Dale has actually scored more goals for Cardiff City than John Toshack. It's true, look it up.

Now I am not a massive collector of autographs these days. My eldest son loves it though. He has all the Inter Cabeltel stars on his Inter v Celtic programme and Katy Hill from Blue Peter. He also has Carl Dale three times, including a memorable occasion when he ran on to the pitch moments after the end of a pre-season friendly at Cwmbran Town. (Oh yes ... we go away to pre-season friendlies, you know.) Anyway, the game had just finished and Carl was a sweaty mess as you can imagine. But far from dismissing my lad with a grunt or a shrug, he patiently signed autographs for Rhys (son) and the growing multitude that soon followed. Such things stick in your mind.

The knee injury continued to plague happy little Carl throughout his time at Parc Ninian, though he remained around the top of the goal scoring charts through, not to make too fine a point about it, an absolutely desperate time in the club's fortunes. If you are a new fan reading this and wondering where Sam will spend his next million, you really cannot contemplate the depths to which the team sank.

For instance, on Sunday 26 November 1995, I set off with my nephew to Edgar Street, Hereford (his first away game). Cardiff City started the match in 91st place. 91st in the league. That's one off the bottom in case you didn't realise. The Hereford programme "Bullseye" picks out Dale as Star Visitor, with "Bullseye Opinion" going so far as to state that Dale's goals were the difference between a bottom club and one "struggling to find a consistent blend". It even predicted that City would escape relegation from the league *provided* Carl Dale remained with the club! That's how bad we were. And that's how good he was. At the time, his goal scoring record for the club stood at 45 goals in 126 games. That's almost a goal every other game since 1991 ... for the second worst team in the league. Bobby Gould later revealed that Dale had been knocking on the door for a Wales B cap in his latter years with City, to go with his call up for the full squad for a World Cup tie against Germany while still a Chester City player. Germany/Hereford United. Hard to connect the two in your mind, isn't it?

So yes, Carl Dale's almost unbelievable goal-scoring feats in a forgotten era, place him firmly up front in my all time XI.

City won that game against Hereford by the way. Carl Dale scored two goals.

11. Nathan Blake

Ah Nathan, how do I love thee? Let me count the ways.

If a computer were asked to come up with an identikit "make-your-own-City-player", I am sure it would produce something not too dissimilar from the simply wonderful Nathan Blake.

Frustration/glee; Attitude/style; Genius/headbanger. All things to all men, he is, for me, all the players we have ever had, rolled into one.

If the agony and the ecstasy of watching Cardiff City over the last thirty years were epitomised in just one man, then it is, Bonnie Prince Nathan of Ringland.

Where to start? From his early days as the most precocious of teenagers, to his poling of a Pole with the sweetest left hook you ever saw at the Millennium Stadium in June 2001 ... can't help loving that man of mine.

I guess the thing is, life is never dull with Nathan around.

On one occasion in the early nineties, I recall Nathan single-handedly destroying Scunthorpe United with a glorious hat trick. As he sprang forward to spring the offside with the deftest of chips for the best of the three, half the field spread itself willingly before him. Gazing into his dark and moody eyes, it cried "take me Big Boy".

Fifty yards and a fourth division goalie between the Great Man and another conquest. He slid forward, as an accomplished lover about to deflower a nervous virgin. I settled back to take in the climax. Wooooosh ... it was over in a trice. Another notch on the Nathan bedpost. I lay back in my seat. Satisfied. Fulfilled, to bask in the afterglow. Nathan turned away, wrote "Fanx Ta Ra" in lipstick on the mirror, and was gone. Away, like a thief in the night.

So many, many times he has brought great joy to the Collins household. My eight-year-old son can name only two footballers, Ryan Giggs ... and Nathan Blake. When Nathan powered in *that* header for Wales against Norway last year, I exploded with glee. "Yes, Yes, YES!" was all I could bring myself to say. For reasons known only to myself, I ripped off my shirt and ran around full pelt, twirling it around my head a la Ryan Giggs in the FA Cup Semi Final against Arsenal at Villa Park. "Get in there my Sonnnnnnn!" I yelled breathlessly, reliving the goal from every possible angle. I swore loudly. I jumped around like a madman. I yelled passionately at the top of my voice in a deafening roar.

Thank goodness, I was only sat at home alone in the living room. What on earth would I have been like in a packed stadium after a shedful of beer?

Of course, I am not alone in such unexplained antics. In 1993 I joined in gleefully with the entire away end at Craven Cottage, Fulham in a rousing chorus of the Nathan Blake song – a game halted for some 20 minutes due to crowd trouble: fights, mounted police on the pitch, the lot. You know the one – "He's black, he's mean. He robs the fruit machine". This was sung with great gusto by all and sundry at the time, though I saw no evidence of Nathan taking offence. In fact, he scored two goals.

His volley against Poland at the Millennium Stadium was greeted with similar acclaim from the 40,000 crowd in 2001. I joined in wholeheartedly of course, despite the fact that I was sat in the Family Enclosure with two kids.

So I have never quite fully understood his reasons for being so put out by the much publicised training ground bust up with Bobby Gould over alleged racist remarks made by the former Wales boss. I guess there's just a time and a place for such things.

Even though he has left us now, he still makes regular trips home to visit the family. My family that is. I took the eldest son to his first ever World Cup game, as Wales beat Belarus in a cracker of a game at a crowded and passionate Ninian Park. The Ninian faithful cranked up the atmosphere with much hwyl. Nathan responded to this great national triumph with a furious rendition of the Ayatollah in the centre of the pitch after the whistle, later explaining that "it just seemed like the right thing to do at the time".

Only once have I been fortunate enough to meet the great man. At Adams Park, home of Wycombe Wanderers, on a Tuesday night for an away game in the Freight Rover Trophy. (I have been to some bloody games I can tell you.) I saw the city players disembarking from their luxury coach, and seized the moment. "Sign the programme please Nathan?" I pleaded, like an excited schoolboy (a 35 year old schoolboy). He oozed slowly down the steps, all the time in the world. I seized my chance. I decided there and then to go for the full, in-depth Parkinson style interview. I was after The Real Nathan. The side the public never see. "Nathan Blake – The Missing Years."

"So, Nathan" I began, "gonna do the business tonight then?" He scrawled something indecipherable across my programme, grunted "'opefully" and was gone. City lost in extra time. Nathan did not "do the business".

Nathan Blake. A legend in his own opinion.

* * *

And so there you have it. What do you think? Willie Anderson knocking in the crosses. Jimmy flicking it on for Carl Dale. Jason Perry and Phil Dwyer in the same defence?

But, I hear you ask: who are these relegation-battling nobodies? How could I leave out Toshack and Clarke; where is Ronnie Bird? Don Murray would surely walk into any All Time City line up wouldn't he. Wouldn't he?

Well, let me put it this way. In 1971 I was only 12. I doubt if I had been to a dozen games before John Toshack left for Liverpool. Whereas between 1975 and 1985, I doubt if I *missed* more than a dozen games. That's bound to affect your choice isn't it.

So when Jimmy Gilligan scores two in two minutes against Swansea, John Buchanan saves us from relegation, or Jason Perry plays on against Barnet with an almighty cut on his head ... well it just leaves an impression.

If you are ten years older than me, you'd probably swap Rod Thomas for Brian Harris, find room for Peter King and Ian Gibson up front and, simply not play Nathan Blake at all.

But do me a favour. If you are going to drop Nathan, can *you* tell him?

6.

The Thin Blue Intifada of Happiness

The 1990s was a curious time for football supporters. The sideburn seventies had sailed in on a wave of post-1966 euphoria, though the gathering masses brought scenes of uncontrolled hooliganism to make a sergeant major blush. Millwall, West Ham, Manchester United and others brought mini reigns of terror to the length and breadth of the country.

In the fashion-conscious nineties, I never saw Cardiff City wear this kit. I use it for painting now.

In time, of course, football hooliganism became something of a national sport, culminating in Heysells and pitched battles all over the continent.

Though largely denied the European stage available to the

Chelseas, Tottenhams and moronic Engerlanders, Cardiff City's loyal band of loonies more than went along with all this and the pages of this book are littered with tales of many a wild antic in the name of Cardiff City throughout this anarchic era.

But the 1990s saw something of a mood swing among football followers around the country.

The 1979 Winter of Discontent, 80s inner city riots and Loadsamonie-yuppie-Youffs had been replaced by Nineties Man: New Man.

Suddenly, it was OK to have a soft side. People started voting for the Green Party. Brit Pop and Acid House preached a retro-druggie love culture. It was even trendy to be Gay.

Football, or "footie" as New Man came to call it, became socially acceptable after a generation of barbarians had almost kicked it to death.

Golden days for fanzines: Contributors included Eric the Red, Karl Heinz-Rumourmonger, Baldrick Schwarzenegger and Nevins Lovechild, allegedly.

Half the country tuned in to see Pearce and Waddle blast England out of Italia 90. All the mums in the north of England wanted to dry Gazza's tears. Those in the south wept for Gareth Southgate six years later.

Amidst this family friendly, surround sound era then, a new breed of football fan emerged. The bare-chested, tattooed madman slowly gave way to, well, not to put too fine a point on it, the Anorak. Or at least, the 1960s replica away shirt. Football was suddenly "cool".

This was fine by me. I was much too spindly for real tattoos and more than happy with a warm anorak on the terraces of Aldershot, Torquay and Brighton. (I got soaked to the skin at Brighton once, but City won 5-3 so, who cares.)

So these anoraks would slowly gather forces around the ground. "Remember that Milk Cup second round

A bargain at just 50 pence: Inspiration for this one was credited to Bob Dylan, The Black Crowes and Van Morrison

Away leg at Gillingham in 1989?" "Yeh – Steve Lynex was booked in the 4th minute but we missed it cos we had left our banner saying 'We're Cardiff, we're barmy, we've had a drop to drink' on the back seat of Wavey Dave's car". Events like this really did happen. Articulate young men could gather in reasonable safety to enjoy high jinks all over the country, while hopeless football teams did battle in dire displays of football, which became almost an irrelevant sideshow. I must tell my friends I thought. In a flash the Fanzine movement was born.

As with everything else of course, Cardiff City fans embraced this new culture with much gusto. Even the bigger clubs only had one, maybe two, fanzines.

Cardiff City had four.

Intifada (the trendy "alternative" one), *Watch the Bluebirds Fly* (comparatively weak but some good jokes), *The Thin Blue Line* (which is still going today and still only 50p I think) and, the one I latched onto – *O Bluebird of Happiness*.

OBOH (worked it out yet?) was run by a trainee journalist and a guy from a Building Society. The publication cycle was a little "unstructured" to say the least, but it was a damn good read when you got it.

I decided to knock up a review of my trip to Oxford to see Jimmy Gilligan's debut for Portsmouth (see "They Brayed in Blue" – a title pinched incidentally from OBOH) and the editorial team loved it. Soon I was a regular, contributing all manner of wacky prose in celebration of the boys in blue.

The fanzine movement typified the 90s – football was fun, the titles were great (we played football matches against fellow mags like *"Dial M for Merthyr"* and Newport AFC's *"Never Say Dai!"*).

I eventually became "nostalgia man", waxing lyrical about fortunes past, long forgotten away trips – and the worst ever haircuts XI.

To continue this chapter, I reproduce now some of my own favourites from these times, complete with editorial comment and backlash. Just think what I was letting myself in for. The first is actually from 1989 rather than the nineties, but hey, it's only a game, right?

*   *   *

Beating the midweek blues – well, nearly

David Collins regains the bug for midweek City travelling, the lure of delightful Birmingham proving too much …

The last 'proper' midweek away game I took in (i.e. not counting Swansea on a Bank Holiday) was against Hereford in 1976. City lost 4-1, John Buchanan scored and a wall collapsed. I hadn't felt the urge since. However, thirteen years is a long time in football and, as my more recent trips had been to such meccas of the game as Sealand Road, Twerton Park, and Penydarren Park (for Merthyr versus VS Rugby), I decided to return to the Big Time. So, it was a case of 'have flexi-time will travel', and it was up to Birmingham City – on Halloween!

Now St Andrew's is not difficult to find, if you know Birmingham. Our driver knew Birmingham like I know Joan Collins and we had a railway guard (Big Adrian) navigating. (Is this a good or a bad thing? – Ed). We passed the NEC twice, went through Solihull (why?) and finally reached the visitors' turnstiles with about twenty minutes to spare. The local plod then directed us to the coach park and left us to walk (unescorted, in Birmingham, at night) to where we'd just driven from.

Still, £4 and we were in.

St Andrew's is massive. Imagine the Bob Bank only bigger, longer and steeper, and that's their home end, stretching right the way along one touchline. Our end was like the old Grange End – huge. The 500 or so City fans had a good view, under cover, from the right hand side of the goal. Executive boxes, seats everywhere, half time scoreboard, the lot. Even with only seven and a half thousand odd people, it was most impressive.

City seemed at home in such quality surroundings and promptly took the lead through Jon Morgan – a firm drive which seemed to take place at least three miles out from the back of our end. Kelly went close, Pike put himself about a bit and Griffith also looked more than useful. Leigh Barnard should have been signed years ago. Roger (Gib) swept it all up at the back and 'Sugar' Ray Daniel did his usual twinkly bits. Brum knocked it about a bit too, so it was even entertaining in patches (heavens, no! – Ed).

This, of course, could not last. After our half-time pie (90p! – the burgers were thirty bob!) Birmingham proceeded to run all over us. Pike looked a shadow of his earlier self, Griffith was never in it and we looked ragged. They equalised but somehow couldn't make it pay. After a few scares, the clock at the far end (I told you they had everything) had crept around to ten past nine. Brum seemed to be settling for a point and a few City players seemed to get their second wind. Rodgerson managed to hobble through the last few minutes and it was all over – 1-1. City had now lost only once in seven games and looked a lot firmer than they did in the 'lost at home to Northampton days' of earlier this season. But they didn't win. Again. We *must* learn to kill off teams when we have the lead. Perhaps a draw at St Andrews is a good result at the end of the day but we draw everywhere! (Not anymore we don't! – Ed). Anyway, three promotions and three relegations (not necessarily in that order) after my last midweek away game, we are back where I left off, down in the Third. Then again, in 1976 Wales was a force in European football, Trevor Brooking's sideburns were a credible and highly acclaimed fashion accessory, and Jimmy Andrews was the tactical guru at Ninian Park. Thirteen years *is* a long time in football.

There you are, not bad for a first effort, eh? A heady mix of news, views and opinion, together with fan-friendly references to the price of pies. I was beginning to develop a taste for this. The writing, not the pies … let's move on. Here's one from a year or so later.

* * *

Crewe are you (August 1991): Crewe Alexandra 1, City 1

A day that promised much and yet, on so many levels, failed to deliver. The first away trip of Rick's Brand New Age. £300,000 worth of new talent. Coach booked well in advance – my mate gets on in Bridgend, keeps a seat for me when I hop on at the station. Pasties, sarnies, the lot. All very civilised.

Unbeknown to us, however, Mike Lambert (Supporters Club top geezer) had elected to send one coach (i.e. my mate's) straight up the motorway, leaving the other (i.e. mine) to do all the pick-ups. I settled down to watch the video ("The Firm" – I ask you, "The Firm"!) next to the fattest man on the coach, thinking that in only about an hour or so I'd join up with the pasties and sarnies at some exotic motorway service station. No such luck. The M5 was chocca. Lambert grew stern. "The George Best Story" and "Life of Brian" came and went. No sign of Crewe. And no sign of the pasties!

Crewe, though, finally dawned. A Fourth Division town if ever there was one. My run of bad luck continued, as I'd forgotten the name of the pub where I was supposed to be meeting Bryn Dobson (fanzine editor) and had to make do with The Royal, one minute from the ground and overflowing with Ayatollahs chanting "We want the Grange End back". In the only quiet corner, I huddled over two foamy pints. There was rugby on the tele. This wasn't going well.

Anyway, once inside the ground, I finally found my mate (minus the pasties) straining to view the proceedings from behind the worst fence in the League – a foot thick, with the top edge cunningly positioned to coincide with wherever the ball happened to be at the time. We squinted hard. We were the ones in blue, and we were all over them. Millar looked strong, Dale and Ramsey were everywhere. 2-0, 3-0, 4-0?

After twenty minutes, though, the storm had passed and Crewe began to drag themselves back into it. A giant banner (see Wales v Germany article in issue 9) was being passed hand to hand along the entire length of the terrace in scenes reminiscent of Italia 90. Well, Crewe 91, anyway.

Suddenly, just beyond the fence, Cohen is clear. He beats the keeper. The crowd leaps. The crowd roars! He must have scored (next time, I'm going in the seats, I tell you). Carl Dale, though, is leading the celebrations, and popular opinion suggests that Cohen has actually hit the post, for Dale to follow up and tap the rebound into the empty net. I am obliged to accept this view of events, and duly celebrate with glee ("Gerroff that fence sonny!")

The goal came just before the interval, and City had looked quite comfortable against a Crewe side that had been scoring a hatful of goals. It got a bit shaky in the second half, though. Abraham has yet to convince me of his match fitness, he's okay in the tackle but his positional play often seems a bit rusty. Gibbins is not exactly yer Continental-type libero in the sweeper's role, he just hoofs it – but hey, this was Gresty Road, and not the San Siro, after all. As for Mark Jones – well, I just don't think he's a full-back. *Phil Bater* was a full-back.

A piece of Jones indecision led to their equaliser, in fact. His failure to hoof the ball a la Gibbins during a Crewe attack, allowed the opposing winger to cross the ball, and their centre-forward to thud home a bullet-like header of which, somehow, I had an excellent view, despite the constraints of the wrought iron fence.

Neither side seemed prepared to bust a gut in search of the winner, though Crewe finished the stronger. Initial dismay quickly dispersed, as we reflected on a deserved away point (happy with a draw at Crewe – whatever is the world coming to?) and gazed with horrid fascination on the sight of Jason Parry doing the Ayatollah.

I scrambled back on the coach and into the sunset, leaving a multitude of transit vans, festooned with flags and banners, to sample the fleshpots of Crewe. We quickly went home. Another ground crossed off the list.

Still, if you thought Crewe sounded bad, stick around. You ain't seen nothing yet ….

These were the start of heady times at Ninian Park. Rick Wright had brought an unprecedented degree of optimism to the terraces, and rumours ran rife that the famous old "sleeping giant" was about to be roused. In truth of course, the giant was merely turning in his sleep and was soon to return to his days of slumber. No matter. We were young, we were foolish. We were desperate!

By now I had been travelling to away games for nearly 20 years, and was slowly turning into something of a Groundhopper. The easy grounds – the Bristols, Swindons, Newports had been ticked off and revisited some time ago, and the glamour trips to fallen giants such as Man City; Wolves and QPR were a thing of the past. Plus, of course, the old "wife and kids" bit had come along now, and long hot Saturdays driving half way across the country weren't so easy to swing anymore. So, it was more midweek travelling. But I surely overdid it at times. Halifax and back on a Tuesday night. What on earth was I thinking of?

*　　*　　*

Remember this one? Me neither.

Halifax of my tears (September, 1991): Halifax Town 1, City 1

As a dozen or so hardy souls waited outside Ninian for the latest fun outing with CCSC, who should appear but Rick Wright. "Off to Halifax are you, lads?" (Dead perceptive is our Rick.) "I've told the lads they've got to do the business tonight." Rick was followed by a number of sharp suited career women types and … two of the quasi-fictitious new seats. Yes they do exist, these were set in wood, one red and one blue. "Can we 'ave all blue with 'Do the Ayatollah' picked out in white letters?" I quipped. Faint smile of non-recognition from the career women.

Twenty seven hours later, we arrived at the picturesque Shay Hotel (God it's a long way!) and then elected for seats in the stand. The Shay isn't as bad as I'd expected. Granted, there are really only two sides and the programme talks of a Football Grounds Improvement Trust grant to "tarmac the away end", but we had a fine view with no obstructive fencing to cope with. Out ran our brave

Bluebirds or rather Yellowbirds. No changes from the side at Blackpool. "Come on City, we can stuff these!"

I then sat through the most ridiculous football match of my life – and that's some claim, I can tell you. The ball was never still, never on the ground and never in the Halifax half. Abraham and Lewis loved it, belting it away at every possible opportunity. Gibbins, surprise surprise, joined in the hoofing at regular intervals. Gavin Ward, though, was superb. Bye bye, Roger.

So much for the rearguard. The City attack had a somewhat more subdued game. But then, goals often come from the least expected quarter. In one less than flowing move, the much abused matchball was bundled forward and somehow landed at the feet of Dale, turning "deftly" he walloped a shot high into the roof of the Halifax net, to the delight of the 100 or so travelling Bluebirds. The 'Barry Blues' banner now hung proudly from a floodlight. (Where are these banners at home games?)

More beer at half time, more 90 mile an hour hoofing it in the second half, more great saves from Gavin. It couldn't last. A free kick to Halifax is, surprise surprise, belted into the box towards the far post, for Richards to nod the ball home. Not a bad goal actually, and the signal for Eddie to replace Pike ("Oh, so Pike has been playing has he?") and Abraham with Heard and Cohen. Minutes later Millar goes down in agony and is stretchered off. Ten men at Halifax on a Tuesday. Imagine it next time you are roaring the lads home in some glamorous once-a-year cup tie. Though poor, it was gripping stuff. Gavin caught everything and Dale burst through towards the end only to be "thwarted" (journalist trained, you see) by a combination of crossbar, defender, pitch, two left feet etc.

So 1-1 it was. Another draw. Hmphh. Clapped the players off, shook hands with Perry. "Well done, Jason son". "Hmphh". Halifax on a Tuesday. Hmphh.

Ah, the fourth division. "As I lay me down to sleep, ... please Lord never let us have to go to Halifax, Crewe and Hartlepool for league games again." But Rick Wright's millions had rekindled my enthusiasm for Cardiff City after years of misery. And, as I say, football was suddenly trendy again. Even "Radio Rugby" (aka Radio Wales) came on board. Here's a winter's tale from a cold and dark December night in 1994. I promise you. It's a classic.

*   *   *

Complimentaries of the Season

Here's a Christmas Tale from Dave Collins as he recalls a cold winter's night hailing from December 2000.

The cold north wind had blown day and night. Inside the humble home, all was quiet. The soft glow of the fairy lights, chestnuts roasting on an open fire, tiny tots with their hearts all a glow ... and me glued to the radio commentary of the Doncaster Rovers v Cardiff City match.

A Family at War huddled around the fireside trying to find the right wavelength ... Radio Wales. My link with the loved ones fighting far from home. You get the idea.

Anyway, these days you can join in on Radio Wales by entering the phone-in quiz. Every time a Welsh club is in league action, Radio Wales goes the whole hog with live commentaries, interviews and the quiz. And lo and behold, yours truly duly made the airwaves on this cold and frosty night. The chance of glory, national fame. A window on the world.

So how did I do? Well, with all due regard for copyright, here's the text of my mastermind performance.

Radio Wales: I presume you are a Cardiff City supporter? (astute, eh?)

Me: That's right, yes. (Good, positive start!)

RW: Do you get much chance to go and watch them?

I mumble something about work commitments, but that I did go to the Caerau game.

RW: A bit of a one-sided affair.

Me: Ah, well! I took my small son who's only three, so we only saw the second half. I remember us losing at home to Weymouth so I was taking no chances.

In full stride now, having nicely established my credentials as a lifelong City fan busily grooming the next generation, I awaited the questions. Five in forty five seconds.

1. Where was John Barnes born?

"Jamaica." (no sweat).

2. Which side is sponsored by Labatts?

"Err, pass."

3. Which Yugoslav played right back for Southampton?

"Umm, pass." (sweat)

4. With which side did Bobby Gould gain an F.A. Cup winners medal?

"Arsenal." (certain)

Wrong (equally certain)

5. Which Scottish manager died at one of his side's games?

"Jock Stein."

Correct

So now they go back over them and with the clock still ticking, they start to give me helpful clues.

Labatts – were bottom of the premier league recently.

"Wimbledon?"

Wrong

Which Yugoslav played right back for Southampton?

"Ivan Golac"

Correct (gasps of astonishment)

Bobby Gould?

"West Brom …, no, West Ham"

Correct

Labatts?

"Forest?"

Correct!

PEEP! The 45 seconds were up, and I've got them all right! A bit of small talk about Jock Stein and Wales' dim World Cup prospects and I'm off the air.

So I now had to sweat even more to see if anyone in the whole of Wales can answer five questions quicker than me. I hold out little hope, but surprise, surprise (otherwise, the rest of the article would be pointless) nobody did. Alright, they only had three more callers, and one of them was phoning from 'The Halfway' pub in Canton, but I'd made it! A Radio Wales winner. Much glee. Millar gives City the lead. More glee. I'd won two tickets for the Wrexham game. A Friday night in December. A night on the town. Yeehaa!

Shall I go on? Come here, there's more! Cut now to the night of the big game. A mouth-watering Welsh derby. It's five thirty and the car won't start. Petrol? Flat battery? We try the jump leads (six o'clock). We change the jump leads (six-thirty).

The battery is declared flat and by ten to seven I'm struggling. I'm standing at the bus stop with forty minutes to get from Llanedeyrn to Ninian Park. The joy of radio glory seems a long way off.

Being in a rush but being at the total mercy of Cardiff Bus is a total nightmare. You just have to stand as time stands still, and then sit as the bus stands still. How does anyone ever get anywhere on time on a bus? I had free tickets waiting to be collected, a mate waiting outside the programme shop for seven o'clock and me running down Wellington Street at quarter past.

Scarf and coat for the winter chill, I'm sweating streams but can't slow down. The dodgy knee is giving way and the clock ticketh on. Time and tide etc etc.

Twenty past seven and I'm drained of all colour, struggling for speech and I've only one knee, but I'm at Ninian Park. Next obstacle please – a queue a mile long outside the main office. Do not pass go. Do not collect free tickets. It must be about 7.27 now and I throw a last desperate roll of the dice, i.e. I cheat. Walking round the head of the queue, I'm able to push past thirty people and knock on the side door (under the Grandstand). Enter Adrian, the Railway Guard from a pub in Birmingham (see OBOH City v Birmingham, circa 1989). Ade knows me. Friends in low places. Tickets duly arrive and I speed up the stairs as the teams take the field. Cracking view. "Come on you blooooooos!"

Now if this was panto, I'd have a happy ending for you. Nathan would return to Never Never Land and never grow up, Baddeley and Abraham would have found their home from the woods and the ugly sisters would sign for Bristol City.

But this, alas, is real life and "Look behind you", City are a goal down. Then a penalty. Ramsey is sure to score. "Oh no he won't"!

Carl Dale and Nathan cry off and the understudies aren't up to it. The baddies have won and Captain Hook (aka Joey Jones) is dancing in the dug out. The Christmas bells rung out – "Jingle Bells, Jingle Bells, Jingle all the way, Oh what fun it is to see Wrexham win away." I hate bloody carol singers.

So to sum up, the car's broke, my knee's broke, promotion's off the rails, Carl Dale still isn't back, all the programmes were sold out and I've got to walk back down Tudor Road.

Thank you for calling Radio Wales.

Bah, humbug!

*   *   *

Finally, I know you are aching to find out … here goes with that worst-ever Haircuts XI. Yes, this really was how I spent my spare time in the mid-nineties.

The City Haircuts XI

Oh dear, David Collins has been taking a few of his loony pills again and has sadly come up with the following Cardiff City all star eleven. Bluebird Jones will have a field day when they see this one. If you have any similar sad City elevens you want to see in print, just send them to us and if they're bad enough, we'll print them!

1. Mark Grew

Most "Wannabees" have Gazza or Elvis haircuts. So what's the fascination with Herman Munster, Mark?

2. Mike Ford

All the photos I've got of Mike Ford give him 12 spikes on the top and nothing anywhere else. Hair by Flymo.

3. Steve Derret

Like something off Star Trek – boldly going where no full back has been before – or since (like Europe, the top of the Second Division etc).

4. Steve Tupling

Longer hair than my wife but a lot less gifted on the ball.

5. Dave Roberts

The only man to have a feather cut before, during and after they were in fashion.

6. Wayne Hughes

Imagine Ralph Coates, without the bits combined over the top. The ugliest man ever to play for Tulsa Roughnecks. Some claim.

7. Anyone who looks like David Giles

Like Paul McLaughlin, Paul Giles. Tarki Micallef, Andy Polycarpou. Why was a resemblance to Giles such a criterion for selection in the early eighties? Clearly, they failed to come up to scratch, so we signed the original again.

8. Robin Friday

Mid-seventies huge sideburns, long heavy fringe, dandruff. Dodgy, you might say.

9. Tony Evans

Mr Smooth. Looked like a Greek waiter. Too good to be true.

10. Trevor Lee

See those games you had when you were little, and you made faces, hair and moustaches with iron fillings and a magnet. That's your hairdo, that is.

11. Nathan Blake

Once, I came home stunned and said to my four-year-old son, "Nathan Blake's shaved all his hair off". Why? he said. I felt I had no answer to this.

*   *   *

So did you like them all? The life and times of a raving lunatic? The fanzine movement was simply a joy to behold. Football became fun and life had some meaning again. Sales were high, articles were mini-classics and I was famous for fifteen minutes.

Why can't the lads on the park display the same passion as those on the terraces? If they did, we'd … well, we'd probably be champions of the world.

7.

What's our Song then, Dad?

Nearly up to date now , and I am busy grooming the next generation. I have two sons, Rhys is now thirteen and Dan is nine. Dan supports Chelsea, coz he liked the song they recorded for the 1997 Cup Final. He has shirts, bags, posters, the lot.

Rhys' room is an eclectic mix of Ryan Giggs posters, pictures of Nathan Blake and Welsh language car stickers. He is coming on just fine.

We all went to the Millennium Stadium for Wales v Brazil a year or so ago and little Dan was gutted cos we lost. This is a

Harrods? Selfridges? Guess again.

good sign I thought, he *should* care whether we win or lose. Rhys was mesmerised by the Mexican waves and a Dial M for Merthyr banner.

Rhys is perhaps the more studious of the two. He is absorbed by the minutiae of football following. He is staggered that the "Captain Morgan" sign stayed on the Bob Bank for 50 years; fascinated by club nicknames, but most of all, he is intrigued by football chants.

"You'll Never Walk Alone" is my brother-in-law's party piece. He sings it when he is drunk at parties and everyone loves it. Except my nephew. I have explained to Rhys that his Uncle sings it because he supports Liverpool, yet his cousin hates it … because he supports Man United.

The author's sons, 1999. "Son, you are a City fan – and that's the way to stay."

Rhys is puzzled by this.

So I continued, "Most clubs have their own songs lad. Leeds sing 'Marching on Together'; Pompey have the Chimes; Bristol Rovers sing 'Goodnight Irene'. It goes on and on."

"So what's our song Dad?"

Ah, my boy … now you've gone and done it. Sit back, relax, enjoy the show. Especially for you – the Top Ten Cardiff City songs of all time. Play that Funky music White Boy!

10. Ooh – Ahh – Stantonna!

Ah we lovin' it, lovin' it, lovin' it! Failed to really take off when originally released with the complex lyrics "who needs Cantonna when we've got Stantonna" (early 90s striker Phil Stant to the uninitiated) but raced to the top of the chart in the "Ooh Ah Stantonna" remix. Originally recorded by the Stretford End Singers, the Bob Bank's upbeat cover version gave fitting tribute to our former SAS hero. Also later re-recorded in a Paul Miller dub version.

9. We Want Ten!

An extremely rare track; now deleted but still cherished by collectors. Only released as a Live Version in a long-forgotten 9-0 Welsh Cup victory over Caerau. But hey! Who cares? Nine nil is nine nil, and you don't see it every week! I'd certainly have settled for 9-0 against Weymouth, Bath City, Hayes etc, etc.

8. Son you are a City Fan.

Golden (or rather "Goal-den") oldie from the halcyon days of the Grange End. A romantic tribe of shaven-headed Batchelor Boys. I used to sing this to Rhys when he was young in an attempt to get him off to sleep. It didn't work.

7. Ten men went to mow.

I have often tried to explain to my wife, the appeal of life on the Bob Bank. Huddled together for the common good, roaring on our brave boys to a stirring victory over Carlisle or someone. The applause, the laughter, the unique terrace banter and rapier sharp wit.

She can't see it. She particularly can't see it when the song in question is a children's nursery rhyme. But we heard a group of City fans singing it in the City Centre one night, and a definite spring entered her step. Things are looking up.

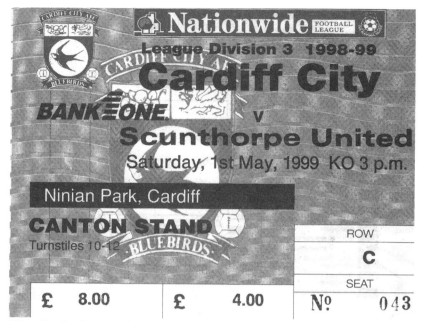

City clinched promotion in this game. Another false dawn. How long
can this last?

6. Dave Bennett, Dave Bennett, Dave Bennett!

Was this man the greatest ever Bluebird? Not the strength of
Dwyer, the glamour of Toshack or even the looks of Keenor.
But eeee, he were rete good that lad. Perhaps his claim to the
ultimate crown may be hampered by the fact that his greatest
feats were performed in the old third version, but then that's
hardly his fault. A loveable and stylish front runner whose
popularity was increased through having a three syllabled
name that fits easily to music. See also "Gary – Gary Bennett
– Gary" which hit the charts around the same era.

5. He Gets the ball an' scores a goal – Jeffrey Hemmerman!

A real stroke of luck this. A star striker with a five-syllabled
name! Ah, what magical names from the past. There's noth-

ing like music for bringing memories of former loved ones flooding back is there?

4. Tony Evans walks on water

And, you know, he could as well. Lightning speed, the deftest of touches and that magnificent kit. I once saw Tony Evans judging a hairdressing competition in some long forgotten Cardiff night spot. I could hardly contain myself. Yet again, the female company was baffled. In a room full of glamorous models and hairdressers, I was jumping up and down at the sight of a mere footballer. They just don't understand do they?

3. You'll never ban a City Ban

The ill-fated voucher scheme of the eighties. The i.d. card of the seventies. Stay away from Derry. Don't follow us to Hereford, says Rick. Twenty City fans at Torquay. Don't let the system grind you down. If Leonard Cohen or Bob Dylan had written a City song, this would have been it.

2. Sam Hamman's Barmy Army

The theme tune of Cardiff City. Been in the charts for a while now, first released in the days of Eddie May. Available at the time as a double A side with the hypnotic "Ooh-Ah, Barmy Army" – now sadly deleted. These days most supporters claim to be "so-and-so so-and so's such-and-such army", but I've yet to come across a song dedicated to any club chairman. But then I've yet to come across anything quite like Cardiff City either. The greatest Barmy Album in the world. Ever!

Rhys has retained a modicum of interest in all this, but I sense he knows I have yet to really answer his question. "So what *is* our song then Dad?" he asks, patiently, Ah, my boy. Only Cardiff City.... *Do The Ayatollah!*

1. The Ayatollah.

Ah, of course. Top of the popstastic mate. Me all time fave rave, me ole china! It would be futile to attempt to analyse The Ayatollah. To ask why Cardiff City fans 'Do The Ayatollah' is to ask why fans support a particular team, why they leap into the air when their team scores, and why it's a disaster when you're relegated. It has just become that thing you do.

The origins of the craze are well documented – see for example 'Phil the Red' in Sigma's "Come on Cymru". Apparently started by just a handful of individuals after a hard night on the cider, the curious ritual has now been adopted as the official password of Cardiff City. New signings are quickly taught its movements and TV and radio commentators rarely fail to mention its more high profile performances.

Basically, there are two versions. In the simplest form, individuals, Players, sections of the crowd etc, are urged to "Do The Ayatollah". The appropriate party is thus obliged to respond with an elaborate two-handed slapping of the head. Both hands together mind, not alternatively. To the first-time visitor to Ninian Park, this can be bewildering. Many a time, I have seen vast hordes of the most boisterous away fans, rendered totally speechless as the Canton End responds to the Bob Bank's pleas of "Canton, Do The Ayatollah, Canton". The sight of several hundred, or even thousand heads being slapped in slow motion unison can appear, on the one hand ridiculous, yet simultaneously hugely impressive. It's right up there with Manchester City's inflatable banana craze or the enormous travelling flags of Serie A. I am amazed that it has not been taken up by others and become a national craze. Secretly though I'm quite pleased that it's still ours.

As I say though, and it is perhaps a little known fact, there are two versions of this manic chart topper. In addition to the "7 inch single version" (blimey, that dates me dunnit?) there is, the original long-form, or, if you like, 12 inch maxi single.

Now this is a complicated mix to put it mildly. Sod Fat Boy Slim. Get him to record the Bob Bank's version of The Ayatollah and see if he can work out the middle rhythm section. He'd soon disappear back to the prawn sarnies and champers of the Premier League I'm sure.

This longer version, which from memory pre-dates the 7-inch cut, has much in common with all great football chants. For example, no-one suddenly stands up on The Kop and announces "Right lads, next up is 'You'll Never Walk Alone'... right 'ere we go... 'When you walk...'. Similarly, there's not a dedicated bare-chested Geordie who counts in a chant of 'Haway The Lads', or even a Jack who decides that now would be a good time to open with a chorus of 'White Christmas' or 'Can't Help Falling in Love'".

Life is much the same at Abbey Road, Ninian Park. For no particular reason, a person of no particular significance will cry "Doooo". Another will respond "Do". Another – yards away perhaps – responds likewise. Soon pockets of randomly scattered individuals are urging simply "Do, Do, Do". In the meantime, the backing singers (i.e. several thousand Cardiff City fans) are slowly raising their arms whilst emitting a gentle moaning-type sound. Then, in an instant – and no-one choreographs this like on MTV or Ant and Dec – the whole choir explodes into a furious cry of "Do The Ayatolla, Do The Ayatollah!" whilst a multitude of heads are slapped furiously with what the South Wales Echo once described as "Islamic type fervour".

Am I making too much of this? Is The Ayatollah or indeed

any other of the songs mentioned above, any better than West Brom's 'Boing, Boing', the 'Pompey Chimes', or Celtic's haunting rendition of 'You'll Never Walk Alone'? Well, of course not. All these songs are – to a greater or lesser extent – unique to the clubs concerned. They carry the emotions, hopes and dreams of a million disappointed football fans. They lure 15-year old school boys to the back of the Grange End and bind their tribes together when accompanying their heroes into combat on battle fields far from home. The 1974 F.A. Cup Final was remembered as much for the off the field contest between 'You'll Never Walk Alone' and 'The Blaydon Races'. In a delicious twist of the football chant culture, travelling England fans taunted the defeated silent Scots fans with cries of "Where's you're famous Hampden roar" in the Play Offs for Euro 2000. It would take twenty minutes to explain the history behind this, suffice to say it is rooted deeply in a terrace culture which stretches back perhaps forty years.

To the uncommitted, all this can seem unfathomably childish. To the partisan, it is marginally short of the very reason for attending football matches at all.

Next time your wife makes you turn the volume down as you watch some noisy encounter from Stamford Bridge, spare a thought for the mindsets of these individuals generating all that noise. Listen for 'Blue is the colour', or 'The Blue Flag', but remember, remember, *only* Cardiff City 'Do The Ayatollah'. Not 'arrff!

8.

This is Tomorrow Calling

Picture the scene. August 2001, the dawn of a brand new season. The years have rolled by, and still, still, I traipse my way to the enormous grey structures of Ninian Park, hoping beyond hope, that one day, one day …

The black and white images of a tram ride from Splott are consigned to the family album. Now it's a 1.8 Rover with built-in CD. The sister's hand knitted scarf is now a forty-quid designer-label-retro-replica-shirt. The frail and timid 10-year old has blossomed into manhood. Wife, mortgage, kids, beer belly. The full monty.

But still, still, the Land of his Fathers calls him home. The football season has started. Much glee. Normal life returns to the Collins household.

The very first day of any new season can lay justifiable claim to the crown of Best Day of the Year. It's right up there with Christmas, yer birthday, Bonfire Night and the last day of school. For just one brief moment, everyone is top of the league. Wigan have the same number of points as Man United. Half the country look proudly on their unblemished home record. The other half are unbeaten away. An early goal at the Reebok Stadium would put Bolton top of the league. Surely the Champions League is now a mere formality? Bolton versus Barcelona. Fulham versus Feyenoord. The dream lives on, year by year.

Yes, the summer was over. The Ashes squandered, football was back. Every year it's the same. Hope springs eternal

– at least until twenty to five, when it's "Sack the Board, Sack the Board". But at Ninian Park this year, this year was different.

Through the long, hot summer of 2001, Sam Hammam had, quite frankly, thrown money at Cardiff City. If the season before had whetted our appetites for Sam and his golden cheque book, his antics during the summer had sent us over the edge, drunk as lords yet thirsty for more.

The club's transfer record – which for years had stood at around £200,000 in a dubious deal with San Jose Earthquakes for Godfrey Ingram – was being smashed (records are always "smashed" aren't they – never simply "broken") with each new edition of the South Wales Echo. The days of £300,000 for Leo Fortune-West seemed an age away as Spencer Prior was signed for £700,000. Yet the new record seemed to last moments, as Graham Kavanagh soon arrived from rivals Stoke City to become Cardiff City's first million pound player. Yes, Cardiff City paid *one million pou*nds for a footballer, in my lifetime. And we were still in only – what I can't get out of the habit of calling – the third division.

Off the field, events had been just unbelievable. A week or so beforehand, I had nipped down to Ninian Park to pick up my ticket for the opening game – against Wycombe. Sales had been going well I had heard – so better safe than sorry.

Well, I hardly recognised the place! Gone the tiny, old shoebox souvenir shop, in its place a glass-fronted, state of the art merchandising megastore. Workmen milled all around putting finishing touches to a host of tiny jobs, the ticket office printed my own personalised ticket with name, address, computer logo – the lot.

But the best surprise of all, lay inside my beloved arena. Sam Hammam, Lebanese tycoon and Prince of Wales, had finally, finally, stuck a roof on the open Grange End. I

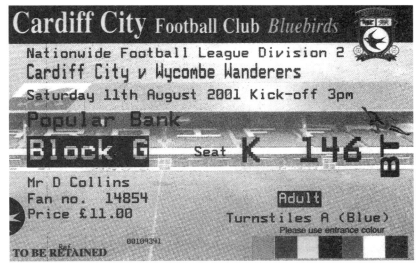

Cardiff City Football Club *Bluebirds*

Nationwide Football League Division 2

Cardiff City v Wycombe Wanderers

Saturday 11th August 2001 Kick-off 3pm

Popular Bank

Block G Seat K 146

Mr D Collins
Fan no. 14854
Price £11.00

Adult

Turnstiles A (Blue)
Please use entrance colour

00109341

TO BE RETAINED

The future starts here ...

blinked back the tears. Cardiff *are* back. Ninian Park was a proper football ground again. God bless you Sam Hammam.

So, on Saturday, 11 August, I parked in my usual Canton car park, just a stone's throw from the ground (literally on some occasions!) and squeezed into my regular watering hole. The Ninian Park public house.

Six deep at the bar, I eventually managed to secure myself a foaming pint of bitter in a floppy plastic glass (why don't they sell Brains SA in this pub?) and "relaxed" in a quiet corner – if such a thing exists in a pub in Canton on match days.

Now, I had a hunch this was going to be a bit special this day. But as I left the pub – a feat in itself – nothing could prepare me for the sight that lay ahead.

Have you ever been to a Premier League football ground, where hot dog vans and geezers selling cheap souvenirs cover every yard of pavement? Well this was CF11 8SX, on the first day of Sam's new dawn. The Sleeping Giant had leapt out of bed, thrown back the covers and leapt bollock-naked into the 21st century. Full colour programmes cried "Season 2001-02, Issue 1". The future starts here.

In the stalls of Sloper Road that day, I could have done *all* my Christmas shopping in one swoop. A Cardiff City Homer Simpson scarf for son Dan (I kid ye not); a "CCFC Kick Ass" South Park hat for Rhys, and for my old buddy Lea who now lives in Epsom, a T-shirt emblazoned with the words "CCFC Money-No-Object-Tour". On the back, it said simply "Be afraid – Be *very* afraid".

Inside the ground – and if it's a while since you have visited Ninian Park I swear to you this is true – there is a pub at the back of the Bob Bank. Cross my heart and hope to die – a *real* pub. Not just a counter where they sell cans of beer, but a proper pub, with barmaids, beer on draught, bar stools and carpets. You could take your wife there – if it wasn't on the Bob Bank.

Needless to say, this bar was completely overcrowded, to the extent to which a sophisticated queuing system had been put in place and you buy beer tokens as you enter the ground. A large gathering milled around inside this cosy tavern, whilst hundreds more occupied some of the huge marquees in the pub grounds. I promise I am not making any of this up. Beer is £2 a pint and the glasses *all* have the Cardiff City crest on. I kept mine and brought it home for Dan as a present. So after another beer (well I had to didn't I?), it was time to clamber to my seat on the mighty Bob Bank itself. Over 17,000 people were at Ninian Park that day. By the feel of things, they had all been in the new pub. Stereophonics and Manic Street Preacher tracks yelled from the PA system. The atmosphere was in danger of becoming overpowering. The enormous Bank of seating urged "Bluebirds! Bluebirds!" The new Grange End was completely full of manic, over-excited zealots. The former family enclosure had been handed over to the club loonies, and amidst all this, a tiny handful of Wycombe fans huddled nervously in a corner. Like startled rabbits caught in the headlamps of a speeding lorry, they stood motionless, no doubt praying that their team weren't about to do anything stupid. Like win.

Tiny cards lay on every seat, in an attempt to recreate a continental style sea of blue around the ground; the noise grew to fever pitch as a procession of flag bearers came out to ring the pitch. The roof nearly blew off the stadium as our million pound man led out our New Age Warriors to a tumultuous welcome. The night's Football Echo wrote "If Wycombe weren't shaken by the incredible welcome given to Cardiff City players, they are strong men indeed".

I turned to my long-suffering mate Dave. Straining to be heard above the din, I shouted, "Excuse me Sir. I wonder if you can help? I appear to be lost. I was looking for Ninian Park!"

* * *

Dave and I go back a long way. I mean a really long way – like Hartlepool, Plymouth Argyle, Chester, Rotherham and Northampton. On that balmy – or maybe 'barmy' – afternoon, Dave was, not to put too fine a point on it, emotional. Tears were close to his eyes as he leaned over to me. "Just think" he said, "all our troubles are over. Never again will we play Doncaster, Barnet and Exeter City. All the false dawns are things of the past. There's no stopping us now. No stopping us!"

He gets a little carried away does Dave, but I knew what he meant. The Handsome Lebanese Knight had truly rescued the Lost Boys from the Never-Never Lands of the 4th Division. We would all, finally, live Happily Ever After.

So Sam's dream was underway, and the media loved it. Barely a day passed without some high profile story of Sam's new antics – "new City signing forced to eat sheep's testicles"; "Sam Hammam soaks reporter"; "Season Ticket Sales Soar!"

Yes, despite the colourful persona, it seems the fans were ready. We really could believe the hype – this was no sequel. Sam pumped his enthusiasm into the club and, as we always truly knew it would, the whole thing simply took off.

It hadn't all been plain sailing for the new Chairman in convincing the fans to follow the dream. The season before, Sam Hammam had launched his dream in a visionary document entitled "Follow The Dream – An Overview 2000". It was radical stuff – new colours, new ground, new name, new badge. South Wales winced collectively. Men in grey suits whispered in corridors. We simply weren't ready for all this.

Sam, to his eternal credit, spent much time then gauging the mood of fans, listening, talking, persuading others to follow the dream – with one or two of the less popular proposals shifted gently – for the time being, at least – to the back burner.

Well I, no doubt, will follow the dream. But I have conditions Sam. To close the story – here are my thoughts on the dream. Dreamer. You know you are a Dreamer. The last pages then, of the diary of a supertramp.

1. The Dream

The dream says, that Cardiff City can be bigger than Liverpool, Manchester United, Arsenal or even Barcelona. The crystal ball has us triumphing over Real Madrid to claim Champions League glory at the Millennium Stadium or San Siro. Hmmm. I'm not so sure. Setting aside the fact that Cardiff City *would*, given a choice of such high profile exposure, miss a last minute penalty to break our hearts in time honoured fashion, I am not convinced. It's a nice idea, but even in the Premier League, Cardiff City v Bolton Wanderers on a Friday night in January? I really don't know. I have spent a lifetime dreaming of the potential of Cardiff City. When I can't get to sleep at nights, I imagine I have pots of money and set about making Cardiff City world beaters. I usually drop off just before Ryan Giggs becomes player manager. It's a long, long way to the upper echelons of the football world. From Barnet to Barcelona - a million miles.

But, to be fair, Sam acknowledges this. All his publicity confirms that it'll take a lifetime. It might not even work at all. But at least – at last – someone has genuinely recognised the potential of Cardiff City AFC and, more importantly, stumped up the cost to go with it. I think we should indulge him just a bit, don't you?

2. The Present

So how far have we got then? At the time of writing, Cardiff City are in the second division. No, I don't mean the *real* second division, like in Toshack, Clarke, Sheffield United etc. I mean the present day Sky TV second division – like in Fortune-West, Cambridge United and the LDV Vans trophy. City limped over the line to promotion last year, don't have a lifeline to Europe via the Welsh Cup and the last game of the season is Tranmere Rovers away. Juventus are going to have to wait a while methinks.

Sam has much work still to do then – he might start by persuading the media in Wales that we are *not* a nation of rugby lovers as they would have us believe. And if he could persuade local commerce and politicians, that top class football in Cardiff really would be a good idea, then he'll be half way there, though perhaps also an old man indeed.

But hey, let's not be cynical here. Cardiff City Football Club has spent millions, and MILLIONS of pounds. We once more sign players I have heard of. You can order tickets over the phone. It's no longer embarrassing to say you support

Cardiff City. We have even overtaken Swansea and Wrexham! OK – they're not Celtic and Rangers, but it's a start.

And just look at Ninian Park these days. The roofing of the Grange End has transformed the ground. Nowadays, Ninian Park once again resembles an intimidating fortress. No longer does the atmosphere drift away over open terracing populated by a hundred fans from Halifax, but is rebounded back from a packed terracing of City diehards – not sure about that feng shui triangle on the top though, but let's not split hairs. I even hear they plan to repaint the Canton Stand roof!

So many of Sam's other improvements have also been much needed for some time. You can now *hear* the PA on the Bob Bank, the burgers smell nice and the shop looks inviting. Yes, though we've still a way to go, things are looking up. What'll be next I wonder? A hotel? Bluebird TV? Sam and Corkey fill in for Ant and Dec on SMTV Live? Hey, you heard it here first – OK?

3. The New Stadium

Perhaps surprisingly, I'm quite in favour of this. Despite the much-needed licks of paint and other improvements, Ninian Park is a football ground from a bygone age.

Strategically placed pillars obscure your view from the Grandstand, fences from the 1970s separate the Bob Bank from the Grange End. Parking is a lottery. There is one hospitality box.

I was at the Madejski Stadium in Reading this season. Gazing around at the covered banks of blue seating, modern media facilities and corporate hospitality facilities, I couldn't help thinking – "yeah, I could get used to this".

But wait, I have conditions. Reading's stadium is arguably the easiest ground to reach in the whole of the league. It's so

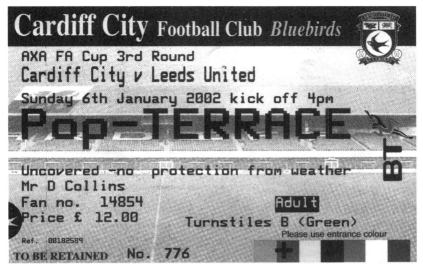

Cardiff City Football Club *Bluebirds*

AXA FA Cup 3rd Round
Cardiff City v Leeds United
Sunday 6th January 2002 kick off 4pm

Pop-TERRACE

Uncovered -no protection from weather
Mr D Collins
Fan no. 14854
Price £ 12.00   Turnstiles B (Green)
Please use entrance colour
Ref. 00182589
TO BE RETAINED   No. 776

Cardiff City 2 Leeds 1: Happy Days are here again?

close to the M4 that my ticket quotes the address as "Junction 11, M4, Reading". I'm not convinced about the "Fosters' Stand" but I suppose I could live with it. No, the main criticism of grounds like the Madejski, is that they tend to be out of town greenfield developments miles out of the centre. Great for away fans streaming down the M4 (I was home by half seven) but less appealing for home fans.

Sam's plans seem to take account of this. Far from locating his new stadium at a motorway junction somewhere between Newport and Bridgend, or even a "brownfield site" down at Cardiff Bay (you can tell I used to work in the Planning offices can't you!), Sam has astutely sited his new empire – yards away from the old one. Inspired.

It'll still feel like "going down the City". I can park in the same streets, drink in the same pubs and still buy Xmas presents from geezers in Sloper Road. But I will gaze out from a space age stadium with my burger in one hand ... and no doubt my credit card in the other.

The Chairman has invited suggestions on a name for our new fortress. He favours monickers like "Land of the Dragon" or "The Taff". Hmmm. I'm not sure about some of Sam's ideas on Welshness – more of which in the next bit – and I think "Land of the Dragon" sounds a wee bit pretentious. He doesn't seem to want to call it Ninian Park, or even, the Ninian Stadium, but he does appear to want to reflect the traditions of our mighty institution.

I wrote to Sam Hammam, suggesting that, if he was eager to capture the proud traditions of the club, yet still capture the Welshness he sought, then he could simply name the new ground "Parc Ninian". As you might have guessed, unless of course dych chi'n rhygl yn yr hen iaith, this is Welsh for Ninian Park. I thought this was ideal, but Sam chose not to reply. Similarly, he also chose not to reply to my suggestion that we pick out the word "Croeso" in seating at Ninian Park (Welsh for "Welcome"), use more Welsh language signage around the ground or even sign a few high profile Welsh language speakers. Oh well, does dim ots, sbo, eh?

4. Wales and Cardiff City

I would say that being Welsh is arguably one of the most important things in my life. You only have to read this book to see that I think. For me, it's right up there with church on a Sunday, worrying about the kids, and Brains SA. To say that I was proud to be Welsh, wouldn't even come close to it.

At every game, I count the number of Welsh players in the Cardiff City line-up. Each May, unless Man United are in the cup final, I cheer for whichever Wembley team has a Welshman in it. It would never occur to me to watch England v Germany on BBC if Wales v Armenia was live on S4C. Similarly, I have limited interest in the Olympics – as I explained to a friend recently, an Englishman rowing a boat means nothing to me.

So naturally enough, I welcome many of the initiatives introduced recently to enhance the 'Welshness' of the club. City have made a stated effort to sign more Welsh players, Welsh flags are displayed prominently around the ground and a red dragon even supports the new advert on the roof. These are visible measures that enhance the club's identity.

Sam has shrewdly spotted the opportunity arising from the club's unique position in Welsh sport. There is almost a captive audience here in Wales, with few other rival attractions, or at least, few with the potential of Cardiff City. The whole of Wales really *would* look to Cardiff City. But, I have my reservations.

As I said earlier, being Welsh is important to me. It is not a joke. Making the players eat sheep's bollocks, having a sheep as club president – I find all this a little offensive. Am I being too sensitive here? Perhaps. But I have had a lifetime watching the BBC ram England, England, England down our throats. Quite frankly, there's more to being Welsh than not being English. Just like there's more to it than coal mines, a few hymns and getting pissed twice a year at rugby internationals. Just watch "Pam Fi, Duw?" if you don't know what I mean. Be yourself. Don't just "not be English". *Editor's note: "Pam Fi, Duw?" – "Why Me, God?" – was a popular Welsh teen soap opera but it currently faces an uncertain future after the death of writer John Owen, who was due in court on charges of child abuse.*

I also have reservations on Sam's well-publicised plans to revamp the club colours, logo and name. I know all this has been well documented, but I can't help thinking Sam's plans are merely "deferred" for the time being, rather than actually ditched. For me, Cardiff City play in blue. Wales play in red. There's no conflict of interest here. City's second colours are

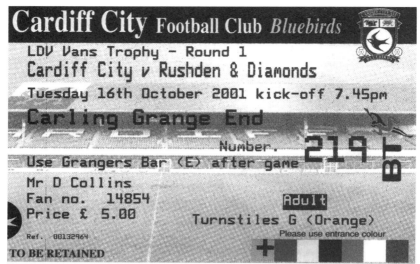

This seemingly meaningless fixture meant that I have seen City play home matches against 90 of the current 92 teams in the League, City won 7-1 – isn't it good when things go well?

yellow. I know it's not original, but they're yellow. Why Cardiff City play in red, or even green, defeats me. Aberdeen are a Scottish club, but I bet their change colours are not navy blue to reflect the national flag? The best way for Cardiff City to promote an image of a confidant, vibrant Wales, is to score more goals than whoever they're playing. Signing the best Welsh talent will help. Juvenile jokes about sheep won't.

5. The author

Ah, the author. Yours truly. So what of me then? What are my dreams, hopes and aspirations?

Well, I guess like many others all around the country, like you if you have bought this book, the fortunes of my football club are central to my whole life. It starts on a Friday, with the local press' preview of the coming weekend's fixtures;

continues into Saturday with the Western Mail; the match itself; Saturday night Football Echo; Sunday papers; Soccer Sunday on TV, and the more reflective mood of the Monday media. Teletext is on permanently in my house. If City lose, it's a tale of woe, if City win, I gleefully snap up all the press copy I can handle. But worse still is if they do not play at all. In the summer, life has no purpose, even mid-winter postponements bring an emptiness which is hard to fill. The armchair fan who supports no-one in particular will be baffled by this.

Over the last few years – indeed over virtually the entire history of this book – Cardiff City have lost more games than they have won. Wales have underachieved dramatically on a national level. My wife says "Why don't you support someone else?" That's a good idea. What about, say, QPR? Nice kit, nice ground in a trendy part of London. Few hooligan problems. Yeah, I'll support QPR. I'll get excited when they win, depressed when they lose, search *their* web site to see how the reserves are doing. "Stand up ... If you hate Fulham. Stand up ...". You just can't, can you?

Some people say there are more important things in life. Sure there are. World peace, third world debt, racial harmony. Not a problem. World peace would be fine – as long as we finish higher than Swansea City.

I don't even really expect the earth from my boys. It might be a while before City win the FA Cup – though teams like Wimbledon, Coventry and West Ham have all won it in my lifetime, so there's always hope.

Sam has dreams of Cardiff City v Juventus in a brand new all-seater stadium. Yeah, sure. That'd be lovely. We need someone with his drive and his ambition. Sometimes I think that if Cardiff City were in the Premier League, all would be well with the world. I could live quite happily chuntering along in the lower half of the Premier League.

To be honest, I'd be quite happy if Cardiff City even just got back to the old second division – and played teams like Wolves, Pompey, Man City and Sheffield Wednesday. Decent clubs, with grounds worth visiting, players I'd heard of and kits I recognise. Hey, we could even win sometimes.

But what do I get? Torquay, Kidderminster and Northampton Town. Away games at Halifax; Hartlepool on a Tuesday night. It's gone beyond a joke. I just want Cardiff City to be a proper football team again.

That's not too much to ask, is it?

More books from
Sigma Leisure:

BEST TEA SHOP WALKS IN SOUTH AND WEST WALES
Dorothy Hamilton
With this guide you will be able to enjoy some of the country's most spectacular countryside and be guaranteed an excellent choice of tea-rooms, all of which have been tried and tested.
Areas covered in the book include the Wye Valley, the Brecon Beacons and Usk Valley, Gower and Pembrokeshire.
£6.95

NORTH WALES WALKING – On the level
Norman Buckley
This book contains 25 circular walks in the hills and mountains of North Wales, intended for those who enjoy gentle walking in fine surroundings, without significant ascents. In addition to the route information and maps, descriptions of towns and villages, landscape and interesting features are all included.
£6.95

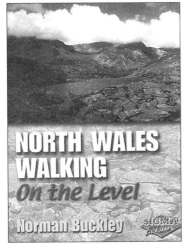

A YEAR OF WALKS: THE WYE VALLEY
Roy Woodcock
The latest in the very popular 'Year of Walks' series, this book describes 20 circular walks in and around the Wye Valley, with a main walk for each month of the year, plus alternative short cuts for most months.
£7.95

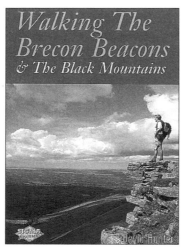

WALKING THE BRECON BEACONS AND THE BLACK MOUNTAINS
David Hunter
This is a collection of circular walks in the Brecon Beacons National Park "... the most comprehensive collection of walks produced for the locality" POWYS COUNTY TIMES. £7.95

WALKS IN MYSTERIOUS WALES
Laurence Main
Ley hunter and researcher Laurence Main has compiled a vast collection of folklore and walks for his readers. "An excellent book" GLAMORGAN GAZETTE. £6.95

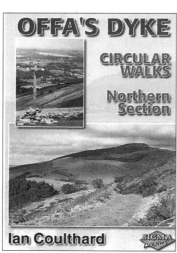

OFFA'S DYKE CIRCULAR WALKS: (Two volumes – Northern & Southern Sections)
Ian Coulthard
Each book contains 25 challenging circular walks based on the Offa's Dyke National Trail from Prestatyn to Knighton. The walks range from 6 to 13 miles, sampling the delights of some of the best hill walking in the country. Both books are required for complete coverage.
Volume 1 (southern section): £7.95
Volume 2 (northern section): £6.95